The Prince and the Plan

The Prince and the Plan

Lead your children to Jesus in 24 memory-making stories

Written & Illustrated by

Sheri Schofield

Carpenter's Son Publishing

The Prince and the Plan

©2018 by Sheri Schofield

Published by Carpenter's Son Publishing, Franklin, Tennessee

Published in association with Larry Carpenter of Christian Book Services, LLC
www.christianbookservices.com

Scripture taken from THE HOLY BIBLE, NEW INTERNATIONAL VERSION®, NIV® Copyright © 1973, 1978, 1984, 2011 by Biblica, Inc.™ Used by permission. All rights reserved worldwide.

Scripture taken from the NEW AMERICAN STANDARD BIBLE®, Copyright © 1960,1962,1963,1968,1971, 1972,1973,1975,1977,1995 by The Lockman Foundation. Used by permission.

Illustrations by Sheri Schofield

Cover and Interior Design by Suzanne Lawing

Printed in the United States of America

978-1-946889-17-1

For Audrey, Asher and Austin

Contents

Introduction

Have you ever wondered, "How can I help my children really understand salvation?" If you have, you are not alone. Explaining spiritual things to children is challenging because children are such literal thinkers. Their world consists of gathering facts and assimilating them, trying to figure out what they mean. Children are told what to do: "Eat your food. Brush you teeth. Go to bed. Don't pull the dog's tail because it hurts him and he might bite you!"

As a group, they tend to not understand similes, metaphors and abstract ideas until they are about eight or nine. Yes, some children do understand these things early. But by eight or nine years of age they - as a group - begin to understand more advanced thought.

Young children ask questions like: "Why can't I see God?" "How do I get my heart out of me to give it to Jesus?" "If Jesus is God, how come he prayed to God?" "Does God have a phone?"

How does a parent answer these questions in ways children will understand?

As a veteran children's ministry teacher, I have learned how children think, how they learn, what works and what does not work. I would like to share with you some of those ideas that have successfully helped children to enter a saving faith. The Prince And The Plan makes it easy for you!

First, let me take you back to your own childhood. What teaching style made the biggest impact on you? Where do your best memories lie? Do you remember a day at the fair or a rodeo? A picnic in some beautiful place? Camping out? Making forts under tables or chairs? These memories stayed with you. They are the keys to unlocking your own teaching abilities.

My earliest memories are from when I was a toddler in the two- and three-year-old class at my church. One part of the classroom was fenced off. Each week a different baby animal was put on display. We would sing a little song about seeing the things God made for us then go visit the baby animals. That year we studied creation and God's love for us. I loved church! It was the highlight of my week.

Later, in kindergarten class, we had table sandboxes with mirrors under the sand where our teacher could brush away the sand to create a lake or river. She would pile up the sand to make hills. She had little, paper characters to move around through the sand as she told the story. Sometimes she would even let us move the characters. What fun! We studied the life and ministry of Jesus that year, and I remember the stories well.

Then came primary class. All of a sudden, the fun stopped. The teacher would tell the Bible story, usually reading from a script. Then we would divide into small groups and go to separate tables, take out our workbooks, and work through a bunch of questions. I did not enjoy that. I remember very little about those Bible lessons. All I remember well is the stuffy smell of the room and the uncomfortable metal chairs.

To be effective, learning needs to be fun! Dynamic! Multi-sensory! And fun is what I bring to you and your children in this book: Fun with a point. These interactive lessons are designed specifically for children ages four to eight years old, though it will also help older children understand the plan of salvation. By reading this book to your children and by doing the Memory Makers, I believe you can lead them step by step into an understanding of God, our need for a Savior, and a lasting personal relationship with Jesus. Those difficult abstract concepts? In this book, I have explained them on a level your young children can grasp.

Salvation is not a formula: It is a personal, saving relationship with Jesus. It is based on trust and commitment to him. I have found that the child who learns all about Jesus and learns to love him, will have a solid foundation for a lifetime of following him. For that reason, I am presenting some key stories about Jesus and how he interacted with people when he was visibly present on earth.

I remember the day I told my children's church class the story of how the religious leaders hated Jesus and tried to stone him. By this time, the children had spent four months learning about how much Jesus loved people, and how they loved him back. When I told the children what the religious leaders tried to do, my entire class erupted in anger! "How can they do that to our Jesus?" "They are very bad people!"

The children were indignant! They had fallen in love with Jesus. There is no better foundation for entering into a saving relationship with him.

This book presents the stories I told to my own children's church class, complete with the Memory Makers and object lessons I used. As you read these stories and pray for your children, I believe the Holy Spirit will produce the same results in their hearts and they will fall in love with Jesus, too.

How To Use This Book

The stories in *The Prince and the Plan* are interactive, designed to help children of all learning styles understand and remember the lessons better. At the beginning of each chapter is a section labeled "What you will need". These are usually very simple, inexpensive items. (If you do not have these items you can substitute many of them.) Make sure you have them before you begin the story.

Read through the story once to identify the "Memory Makers" and other multisensory actions so you will be prepared for them.

Memory Makers have border frames like this, and are easy to find.

Words that are in parentheses and italics - *(like this)* - are directions for the teacher and are not to be read aloud.

If you are using this book to teach a weekly Bible class for children, the Teacher's Guide at the end of the book has suggested songs and a memory verse for each lesson. I have included all the Bible verses supporting the story. There is also a Review Activities section with some suggestions about how to reinforce the lessons. This section requires more time to prepare, but can add significantly to the learning experience.

Children love it when their parent or teacher enters into play with them! By dramatizing the stories through reenactment and "let's pretend", you and your child can develop strong, happy memories together centered on the Bible, God's Word to us.

Chapter 1: How It All Began

(What you will need for this lesson: A Bible, a ball of play dough - any kind of dough or clay will do; a small cup of water for each person; a piece of fresh fruit for each person.)

Forever and ever before there was a sun or moon or stars . . .
before there were mountains and lakes and trees . . .
before there were people . . .
before anything was created . . .
there was God.

Nobody knows what God looks like because God is a Spirit. Our eyes are not powerful enough to see spirits. But God wants us to know him! He told some people called prophets to write down things about him for others to read. We now have God's words in a special book called the Holy Bible. *(Hold up the Bible.)* These words are true.

The Bible tells us that God is light. There is no darkness in him at all. You know how bright the sun is? Well, God is brighter than that! He is so bright that people cannot look at him, just as we cannot look at the sun without hurting our eyes. So God does not let us see him.

There is only one God, but he is three Persons: God the Father, God the Son, and God the Holy Spirit. God the Son's name is Jesus. Each Person of God has a special job to do. We pray to God the Father in Jesus' name, and he answers our prayers. God the Holy Spirit comforts us when we are sad. He teaches us the things the Father wants us to know. God the Son, Jesus, is called the Prince of Peace. The Prince did something very wonderful for us. We will learn more about that in these stories.

Memory Maker: How can God be three in one? *(Show ball of play dough)* This is a ball of play dough. If I break part of it off *(demonstrate)*, is it still play dough? Yes! If I break off another part, is it still play dough, too? Yes! Now let's put it back together. See? It is just one piece of play dough now. That is how it is with God. He is one God, but he is three Persons. All three Persons of God share one loving heart. *(Shape play dough into heart shape.)* That loving heart of God loves you and me so much! He even sends his angels to watch over us!

God wants us to talk with him. When we talk to God, we don't need a phone. All we have to do is pray. God always hears us, even when we whisper. He will always answer us in the way that is best.

God is always good. God lives in a beautiful place called Heaven. Nothing bad can live there. God the Father's throne is at the center of Heaven. Angels fly around his throne calling out, "Holy! Holy! Holy is the Lord God Almighty!" Holy means perfect and wonderful and very special. God is perfect in every way.

God is always fair. He always does what is best, even though it may not always feel that way. God sees and hears everything all the time. God is the most powerful force that ever was or ever will be. Nobody can fight God and win! God watches over everyone who loves him. When bad things happen sometimes to those he loves, God turns it into good.

Someday God will bring his throne to earth and live with us. When he does, there will be a spring of water coming from God's throne called the Spring of Life. From the spring will flow a great river called the River of Life. It will be clear as crystal. It will flow down the middle of the main street in front of God's throne. Anyone who drinks from the River of Life will live forever!

Memory Maker: Let's pretend we are drinking from the River of Life! (*Serve each child a small cup of water. Drink together.*) Mm! Isn't the water good!

There will be a great tree that grows on both sides of the river. It is called the Tree of Life. The leaves from the tree heal everyone. The tree is very special: It has twelve different kinds of fruit every year, a different fruit for each month.

> **Memory Maker:** Let's pretend we are eating some fruit from the special tree! *(Give each child a piece of fruit.)* Yum! Isn't it good? Let's thank God for making a special place called "Heaven".

Prayer: Close your eyes so you can think only about God while we talk to him. I'll say something, then you say it after me: Dear Father God in Heaven, we are so happy to learn about you! We are glad to know that you are powerful and strong and that you love us so much. Please help us live for you today, and to always love you, too. In Jesus' name, amen.

Chapter 2: Creation And Hearts

(What you will need for this lesson: pieces of fruit for a snack for each child.)

Review: In our last story we learned about God. Can some-one tell me what you learned? *(God is Light, there is no darkness in him at all. Angels fly around God's throne saying, "Holy, holy, holy is the Lord God Almighty." Someday God's throne will be here on earth. There will be a special spring called the Spring of Life that becomes the River of Life. Whoever drinks of it will live forever.)*

Lesson: In the beginning, God created the heavens and the earth. Earth is in a galaxy of stars called the "Milky Way". Earth is just a tiny, blue dot way out near the edge of the galaxy. There are billions of stars in the Milky Way. When the sky is clear at night, we can go outside and see some of them.

God made the sun, moon and stars for lights. He made air for us to breathe. He made birds and fish and animals. He created the first man and woman, Adam and Eve. He made a beautiful garden called "Eden" where they could live. Adam and Eve took care of the garden and the animals.

Adam and Eve didn't wear clothes. Since none of the animals wore clothes, they didn't even think about it.

When God created Adam and Eve, he gave them something special, something that none of the animals had. He gave them an extra heart. The first heart was the body-heart. The body-heart pumps blood to the arms, legs, fingers, toes and head. Animals have this kind of heart, too. When you run fast then stop, you can feel your body-heart beating inside you. You can put your hand on your chest and feel it pumping.

Memory Maker: Let's try to make our body-heart pump so we can feel it. *(Do some exercise like jumping jacks or running in place, then stop and feel the heart beating.)* That thump-thump-thump is our body-heart working for us.

The second heart - the extra one - is our soul-heart. A soul-heart is the invisible part of us that makes us who we are. Doctors cannot find it. It is not in our hands or feet or arms or legs. It is something inside us that makes us feel and think and love.

We feel our soul-heart when we are sad or happy. When we are sad, we say, "My heart is breaking," or, "My stomach feels heavy."

When we are very happy, sometimes we feel like there are butterflies in our stomach. That is our soul-heart we are feeling. When we say, "I love you with all my heart," we are describing how we feel in our soul-hearts that God gave to all humans. With our soul-hearts, we talk to God when we pray. When the Bible talks about our hearts, it means our soul-hearts.

While the body-heart can stop and the body can die, the soul-heart keeps living. In these stories, we are going to learn what happened to people's soul-hearts.

God loved Adam and Eve so much! Every evening he would come to the garden and talk with them. Adam and Eve had very good times together with God. But did Adam and Eve love God?

God does not make anyone love him. That is something each person has to choose on his own. So God gave Adam and Eve a choice. What would they do with their soul-hearts? Would they choose to love God? Or would they go their own way?

There were many fruit trees in the Garden of Eden that had delicious fruit on them. God told Adam and Eve, "You may eat the fruit of any tree in the garden ... except this one." He showed them the special tree. "This is the Tree of the Knowledge of Good and Evil," God said. "Do not eat its fruit! The day you eat it, you will die."

God was giving them a choice to see if they loved him. If they trusted and obeyed God, it would show that they did love him. But if they did not obey, that would show that they did not love God enough.

For some time, Adam and Eve obeyed God. They trusted him. They showed that they loved him.

Memory Maker: Let's eat some good fruit, the kind that God said Adam and Eve could eat in the garden. *(Hand some fruit to each child.)*

But there was a problem. The problem started when something bad happened in Heaven, the place where nothing bad could stay. One of the angels was very bad. He and some of his angel friends started a war in heaven.

But God's good angels were stronger than the bad angels, and Michael, the good leader of God's angel army, threw the bad angels out of heaven. The leader of the bad angels is named "Satan". The Bible calls him "the devil", too. Satan is mean, he is cruel and he is a tricky liar.

After Satan was thrown out of Heaven, he came down to earth. He knew that God had created a beautiful, perfect world. He knew that God wanted to see if Adam and Eve would love, trust and obey him. Satan knew about the Tree of the Knowledge of Good and Evil, and Satan had a plan that would make God very sad.

In the next story, we will discover what happened.

Prayer: Dear Father God in Heaven, thank you for making such a beautiful world for us. Help us to choose to love you always, and to remember to thank you for taking care of us. In Jesus' name, amen.

Chapter 3: The Choice

(What you will need for this lesson: a whole fruit like an apple or plum; a small container with a lid; small paper hearts - about 2 inches high - for Adam, Eve, and one for yourself and each member of your class - write Adam, Eve, your name and the name of each of the children on hearts -- have a few extras in case you need them. You will need to save the container and hearts for future illustrations.)

Review: In our last story, we learned that Satan went into the Garden of Eden to do something to make God sad. Satan was a spirit and didn't have a body like people and animals have. He wanted to get Adam and Eve to disobey God! Today we will discover how he did that.

Lesson: Satan decided to get inside a serpent in the garden. We don't know exactly how serpents looked in the Garden of Eden, but we do know they did not crawl on the ground. They may have had wings and feet. The serpent was near the Tree of the Knowledge of Good and Evil.

When Adam and Eve walked through that part of the garden, the serpent called out to Eve. Through the serpent, Satan asked Eve, "Did God say you would die if you ate the fruit in the garden?"

"Oh, no," Eve said. "We can eat the fruit from any tree in the garden except for this one. God said we should not eat it. We shouldn't even touch it or we'll die!"

The serpent hissed, "You will not die! God knows that when you eat it, you will become like gods. You will know good from evil!"

Eve began to wonder about God. Was God telling the truth? Now Eve had to choose whom to believe. Would she choose to love and obey God? Or would she choose to believe the serpent?

Eve decided to believe the serpent and to disobey God. The Bible calls this "sin". Eve picked a piece of fruit from the Tree of the Knowledge of Good and Evil. *(Hold up fruit.)* She took a bite. *(Take a bite of the fruit.)* Adam watched Eve. He saw that she did not die.

Eve handed him a piece of fruit and he ate it, too.

Neither Adam nor Eve died! Had God lied to them? No! Their bodies did not die right away, but they started dying the moment they ate the fruit. It would take many years, but because they had disobeyed God, their bodies would someday die. That was part of the punishment for disobeying.

But something else did happen right at that moment. Adam and Eve suddenly knew that they were naked! They thought, "This is bad! How can we fix it?"

They found some big leaves in the garden: fig leaves. They sewed the leaves together and made clothes out of them. The leaves were scratchy!

That evening when God came to visit them in the garden, Adam and Eve hid from him. "Adam? Where are you?" God called.

Adam and Eve came out of their hiding place. "We were naked, so we hid," Adam said.

"Who told you that you were naked?" God asked. "Did you eat fruit from the Tree of the Knowledge of Good and Evil?"

Adam and Eve nodded. Adam blamed it all on Eve. "She gave me the fruit!" he said. Eve blamed it on the serpent.

God was very sad. He knew what would happen. Adam and Eve would die. Their hearts, the invisible part inside their bodies that made them who they were, would go on living even after their bodies died. Because they were now bad on the inside, they could never go to God's beautiful city of Heaven. They had become slaves of Satan, God's enemy. They would have to stay with Satan forever! They were caught in the Sin Trap.

Memory Maker: *(Show small container with lid.)* Let's pretend this is the Sin Trap. When Adam and Eve disobeyed God, their soul-hearts were caught inside the trap. *(Place "Adam" and "Eve" heart cutouts into trap, then put lid on container.)* Everyone born after Adam and Eve was born in the Sin Trap. I was born in the trap. You were born in the trap, too. *(Place hearts with your own and each child's name in the trap, and close the lid.)* No matter how hard we try, nobody can open the trap from the inside. In the trap, people do all kind of things that make God sad. They tell lies, they fight, they steal and lots of other bad things. God calls this "sin". We sin because we are born inside the trap.

But God loved the people of Earth so much! He wanted to rescue them from Satan and all the bad things in the Sin Trap. The Bible tells us that before God created the world, he knew that people would disobey him. So God already had a Rescue Plan prepared for us. In our next story, we will learn something about God's plan.

Prayer: Dear Father God in Heaven, thank you for loving us. Help us to trust and obey you always. In Jesus' name, amen.

Chapter 4: God Plans A Rescue

(What you will need: The Sin Trap; paper, crayons, pencils; a scroll made from paper with these words on it: Promised One, virgin, Bethlehem, star.)

Review: In our last story we learned that Satan tricked Adam and Eve into eating fruit from the forbidden tree. Do you remember what happened to Adam and Eve's soul-hearts? *(They were caught in the Sin Trap. Show Sin Trap.)* Because of Adam and Eve, everyone is now born inside the Sin Trap. But God wanted to rescue us!

Lesson: Adam and Eve had chosen to disobey God and to go their own way. God knew that they could no longer live in the Garden of Eden. There was another very special tree in the garden called the Tree of Life. God knew that if they ate from the Tree of Life, they would live forever, and they would become more and more evil every day. He would not let that happen!

God looked at Adam and Eve. He knew the fig leaves they wore would soon fall apart. So God made clothes out of animal skins for them. Yes, some animals had to die in order to make the clothes.

Then God sent Adam and Eve out of the Garden of Eden and placed an angel at the gate to the garden. The angel had a flaming sword. He was not to let Adam and Eve back into the garden.

God told Adam, "You will have to work very hard from now on. Food will not be easy to grow like it was in the garden." He told Eve, "You will have a lot of children from now on, and it will be difficult. You will want to boss your husband, but he will be your boss."

God punished the serpent, too. From that time on, all serpents, or snakes, would have to crawl on the ground. God knew that Satan was behind this disobedience. He said to the serpent, "I will make you and the woman enemies. All the people who come afterward will be your enemies." Then God gave the serpent a clue about something the Prince of Peace would do. He said, "You will bite his heel, but he will crush your head." What did God mean? Ah! It was a mystery!

Adam and Eve were now separated from God. But God loved them and he had a plan to get them back! He would send the Prince of Peace to Earth on a special rescue mission to save the people he loved so much. The Prince would rescue Adam and Eve and everyone who wanted out of Satan's trap. Not even the angels knew about the plan! It had to be a very big mystery, because if Satan found out about it, he would try to mess things up.

Even though Adam and Eve were in trouble with God, he promised to rescue them from Satan someday. That gave Adam and Eve hope, and they believed God's promise.

It would be many years before the Prince of Peace would come to earth. People who believed God called him the "Promised One", the "Messiah". They knew that someday God would send the Promised One to earth to rescue them.

Every now and then, God would give people a clue about this special Person. The clues were called "prophecies". The prophets would write the prophecies on scrolls for people to read. *(Show scroll. Untie it and unroll it.)* The Promised One would be born of a virgin, a girl who had never lived with a man like mommies and daddies live together. He would be born in Bethlehem. God would put a special star in the sky over the place the Promised One was born. The Promised One would be a great king. There were lots of clues, but nobody could figure them all out. And neither could Satan, God's enemy.

The people who loved and trusted God did not know when the Promised One would come, but they still believed. Someday, God would rescue them from the Sin Trap.

Prayer: Dear Father God in Heaven, thank you for your plan to rescue us from the Sin Trap. Thank you for the Prince of Peace. Help us to trust you and obey you today and always. In Jesus' name, amen.

Memory Maker: Let's make scrolls today. *(Hand out paper, crayons and pencils.)* Write or draw something about the Promised One. Here are some words you can copy from my scroll. *(Place your scroll on activity table)* Do you want to draw a picture of the place the Promised One would be born? What do you think Bethlehem looked like? Do you want to draw a picture of the star God would put in the sky? You choose. *(When children are finished, roll up their pictures and tie them like scrolls.)*

Chapter 5: The Rescue Begins

(What you will need: The Sin Trap; a pitcher or large, clay jar)

Review: The last story we read told us about the Sin Trap and how Adam and Eve disobeyed God and their soul-hearts were caught in Satan's trap. Because of that, everyone was born inside the Sin Trap. But what did God promise? *(He would someday send the Promised One to rescue everyone from the Sin Trap.)*

Lesson: A long, long time passed after the Garden of Eden. Many more people were born on the earth and many things happened. But finally it was time. The Prince of Peace was ready to come to earth! When the Prince made his great plan, he was still a spirit, like God the Father. He would need a human body in order to save people from the Sin Trap. *(Show Sin Trap)* How would the Prince get a body? Let's find out!

In the little town of Nazareth, in the land of Israel, there lived a girl named Mary. She was kind and sweet and she loved God very much. She believed that God would someday send the Promised One. But she didn't know how or when he would come.

Back in Mary's time, people did not have running water in their houses. Every morning the women of the house would take big, empty jars down to the well *(show jar)*, fill the jars with water, put the jars on their heads or shoulders *(demonstrate)*, and carry them back up to their homes. Usually, the town was built on a hill, and the well was at the bottom of the hill. It was hard work!

Mary was engaged to a man in Nazareth named Joseph. But they were not married yet. Joseph was a carpenter. He helped build houses and furniture. Mary loved Joseph and was looking forward to being his wife.

One day, God sent his special angel, Gabriel, to talk to Mary. When Gabriel appeared, Mary was afraid! She had never seen an angel before. Why would an angel want to talk to her?

Gabriel said, "Hello, Mary! Don't be afraid! God likes you a lot! You are going to have a baby boy. He will be great, and he will be called the Son of God. He will be a great King, and his kingdom will never end."

"How can this be?" Mary asked. "I am not married!"

The angel said, "The Holy Spirit will put the baby in you. That is why he will be called the Son of God."

Mary was very surprised! But she said, "Okay. Let it be the way you said."

Then Gabriel disappeared.

Mary was so excited! She was going to be the mother of the Promised One!

Memory Maker: Let's pretend we are working with Mary. Here's a little rhyme we will say together *(make up simple hand motions to go along with rhyme; repeat it 2 or 3 times):*

Mary, Mary, fetch the water. Mary, Mary, make the bread. Mary, Mary, see the angel! Hear the words the angel said! Mary, will you be the mother of God's one and only Son? Mary answered, "Yes, I will!" So Jesus came, the Promised One.

When Joseph heard that Mary was going to have a baby, he was sad. He didn't know about the angel. He loved Mary. But he thought, "I cannot marry her. This is not my baby."

But when Joseph went to sleep that night, the angel of God appeared to him in a dream. "Joseph," the angel said, "Don't be afraid to take Mary as your wife, for the baby she will have is from the Holy Spirit. Mary will have a Son, and you are to give him a special name: Jesus, which means "Savior", for he will save his people from their sins."

Joseph was excited, too! He was going to get to help Mary raise this special baby! What a great gift from God!

Joseph told Mary about the angel in the dream. Mary told Joseph about the angel who had talked with her. Wow! They were chosen by God to raise his Son, the Promised One!

So Joseph took Mary home as his wife. He loved her very much and Mary was happy, too, for she loved Joseph. But Joseph did not live with Mary as a husband until after her baby was born. This was so the Bible prophecy, one of the clues about the Promised One, would be proven true. It was the clue that the Promised One would be born of a virgin.

Prayer: Dear Father God, thank you for loving us so much that you sent us your Son, Jesus, the Prince of Peace. In Jesus' name, amen.

Chapter 6: What Happened At Bethlehem

(What you will need: A baby doll wrapped in a small blanket and placed on a pillow in a box or hamper. Hide the doll before you read the story. Bring pillows into the room where you are reading and set them aside. You will pretend these are sheep during the Memory Maker time.)

Review: Whom did we learn about in our last lesson? *(Mary & Joseph)* What did the angel ask Mary? *(Will you be the mother of God's one and only Son, the Promised One?)* What did Mary say? *(Yes.)* Did an angel talk to Joseph and tell him about the baby, too? *(Yes)* So Mary went home to Joseph's house, but they did not live together as man and wife until after the baby was born.

Lesson: In the days of Mary and Joseph, Caesar Augustus was the emperor, the ruler of the whole world. About the time Mary was almost ready to have her baby, Caesar sent out a new law: Everyone must go to their hometown and be counted for Rome. Joseph's hometown was Bethlehem, the town where King David had been born. People called it the City of David.

It was a long way to Bethlehem, so Joseph and Mary needed to take food and clothes with them. Joseph would need his tools so he could find work.

"We will have to stay at the inn for a while," Joseph said. The inn was what we usually call a motel.

But when Mary and Joseph arrived at the inn, there were lots of people and carts and animals there. "Let's go knock on the door," Joseph said, helping Mary get down from the cart.

"I think the baby is going to come very soon!" Mary said. "I hope there is a place where I can have him without everyone else around."

Joseph knocked on the door. He could hear all the noise inside. Did the innkeeper hear his knock?

Suddenly, the door opened. The innkeeper saw them. "Oh, dear!" he said. "The inn is very full. I don't have any more room!"

"Isn't there any place for us to sleep?" Joseph asked. "As you can see, my wife is about to have a baby, and we need a private place for that."

The innkeeper said, "Well, there is no room here in the inn, but if you are willing, you could find a place in the stable."

That night, Mary's baby was born. Joseph held the little baby boy in his arms and said, "Your name is Jesus! You will save your people from their sins, just like the angel said."

Mary washed Baby Jesus and wrapped him in clean clothes. In those days, they didn't have diapers. They just wrapped the baby around with cloth called "swaddling clothes". So God's Son, the Prince of Peace, was not born in a palace with lots of people to welcome him. He was born in a stable, with cows and donkeys all around.

Joseph found a manger, a big box with hay in it. "This manger should be a good, safe place for Baby Jesus to sleep," he said.

Mary gently laid Baby Jesus on the hay in the manger. He was so sweet! He was so tiny!

That night God did two things to announce that Baby Jesus had been born. First, he put a bright star in the sky over Bethlehem. Then he sent some of his angels out to a field where some shepherds were watching over their sheep.

The first angel suddenly appeared to the shepherds. The dark sky was filled with bright light! The shepherds were very afraid! But the angel said, "Do not be afraid. I bring you good news of great joy that will be for all the people! Today in the town of David a Savior has been born to you: You will find a baby wrapped in swaddling clothes and lying in a manger."

Suddenly, lots of other angels appeared with the first angel. They shouted, "Glory to God in the highest, and on earth peace to men on whom his favor rests!" Then the angels disappeared.

The shepherds could hardly believe what had happened. "Wow! Did you see that?" they said to each other. "We have got to go see this baby!"

The shepherds left their sheep and raced into Bethlehem. They looked in the stables around town until they found the one with Mary, Joseph and Baby Jesus. "Yes! It's the baby the angel told us about!" they said when they saw Jesus lying in the manger. They knelt down and worshipped the special baby, the Promised One.

Memory Maker: Let's pretend we are shepherds watching over sheep. Let's pretend these pillows are sheep. It is nighttime. *(Turn out the lights.)* Everyone except one shepherd is asleep. That shepherd is watching over the sheep. *(Lay down on the floor next to the pillows. Pretend to be asleep for a while, then turn on the light.)* Oh! Look at the bright light! There's an angel! What is the angel saying? *(Have children repeat the angels' message.)* Let's look for the baby in the manger! *(Search the house/room together until you find the baby doll in a box.)*

Prayer: Dear Father God, thank you for sending us your Son, Jesus. Help us to learn all about him so we can be free from the Sin Trap. In Jesus' name, amen.

Chapter 7: The Wise Men

(What you will need: A piece of paper rolled up like a scroll and tied closed with a ribbon or string - on the paper, write the words "A star will come out of Jacob, a scepter will rise from Israel"; two different kinds of perfume; a bag of coins; a blanket and two pillows; baby doll; basket or sack containing bread, cheese, juice for the children.)

Review: We learned in our last story that Joseph and Mary traveled to the town of Bethlehem. When they arrived, could they find a room at the hotel or inn? *(No)* The innkeeper said there was room for them where? *(In the stable)* So Jesus was born in a stable, with horses and cows and goats and other animals all around. Did God send angels to tell the rich people about the baby? *(No. He sent the angels to shepherds.)* Did the shepherds go worship Baby Jesus? *(Yes)*

Lesson: The same night Jesus was born, God put a special star in the sky. It was very bright. Many years before, God had given people a clue: this star would tell everyone that the Promised One had come. Far away in the east, some wise men were looking at the night sky, studying the stars.

"Look!" said one of the men. "There's a new star in the sky!"

"Yes, there is!" said another. "I wonder what this new star means?"

Another wise man said, "You know, I remember reading about a special star that would appear. Now where did I read about it? It's somewhere in my ancient scrolls."

The next day, the wise men started looking through all their scrolls. They didn't have books like we do. In those days, people wrote on animal skins or a very old kind of paper made out of reeds.

Memory Maker: *(Show scroll)* They rolled it up like this. The wise men had collected a lot of scrolls. It took them a long time to go through all those writings. Then one day, one of the wise men found something about the special star in a scroll. *(Open scroll and read it - or have your older children read it.)*

What did it mean? The wise men knew that the verse meant a great King had been born in the land of Israel, the land belonging to the descendants of Jacob.

"Let's go find this great King!" one of the wise men said. "Yes!" said the others. Someone said, "We should take him expensive gifts, too!" So the wise men bought special gifts: gold, frankincense and myrrh. Frankincense and myrrh are perfumes. They smelled really nice.

Memory Maker: *(Bring out two different perfumes and let the children smell them.)* These perfumes are not frankincense and myrrh, but they smell good, just like the ones the wise men bought. *(Show bag of coins.)* They also brought gold for the new King. We don't have gold, but we have money we can pretend is gold.

The wise men traveled across mountains and deserts following the special star. It was two years before they reached the land of Judah in Israel! "Where would a new King be born?" they wondered. "Of course! He would be born in a palace! Let's go to the palace in Jerusalem and ask about the new King there." So they went to Jerusalem and asked if they could see the king who was in charge then.

Herod was the king of Judah in those days. He was a very wicked man. When the wise men came to him, they asked, "Where is the newly born King of the Jews? We have come to worship him!"

Herod was angry! But he pretended to be interested. He called in his own wise men and asked them where the baby would be born. They said, "He will be born in Bethlehem, O king."

Herod told the wise men, "Go to Bethlehem and find the baby. Then come back and tell me where he is so that I can go worship him, too."

Do you think Herod wanted to worship Baby Jesus? No!

The wise men got on their camels that night and they followed the star to Bethlehem. There they found Jesus with his parents. By now, Jesus was about two years old, and his parents no longer lived in a stable. They probably had their own house. The wise men came inside and put their special gifts in front of Jesus and worshipped him.

That night an angel told them in a dream to leave, to go back home, and not to tell King Herod where Baby Jesus was. So the wise men left.

Then the angel awakened Joseph. He said, "Wake up! Joseph, King Herod wants to kill Baby Jesus! You are to take Mary and the baby to Egypt!"

Joseph woke Mary. It was a long way to Egypt, and they would need many things for their journey. They probably put everything into a cart pulled by cows.

Memory Maker: Let's pretend we are with Mary and Joseph and Baby Jesus. Let's be very quiet so we don't awaken anyone in town! *(Spread blanket on floor; put two pillows on one end - these are pretend cows.)* Let's pretend this blanket is our cart and these pillows are cows. Now, let's pretend to load our food and blankets into the cart. Put the jars and pots in, too. Let's get some firewood! Someone bring Joseph's tools to the cart. *(Put basket or sack of real food into cart, too.)*

Ok, let's have Mary and Joseph and Baby Jesus ride in the front of the cart, and Joseph can drive the cows. *(Let Mary hold the doll.)* Shhh! Let's get into the cart now. Let's drive out of Bethlehem very quietly. The road is rough. *(Pretend to bounce)* Shhh! We are almost out of town! We travel and travel. Finally, it is morning. Are you hungry? I think Mary and Joseph and Baby Jesus are hungry. So let's stop and have breakfast. Everyone get out of the cart. Let's have a pretend fire here by the cart so we can get warm. *(Hand out food and juice.)* Mm! Food sure tastes good this morning! I'm glad Baby Jesus is safe now!

Prayer: Dear Father in Heaven, the wise men brought your Son special gifts. We want to bring him a special gift, too. We bring him our hearts. We want Jesus to live in our hearts and teach us how to love and obey you. In Jesus' name, amen.

Chapter 8: What Jesus Learned In School

(What you will need: white, fluffy batting or wool; colored yarn)

Review: About two years after Jesus was born, who came to worship him? *(Wise men.)* Was King Herod happy to learn about Baby Jesus? *(No. He wanted to kill Jesus.)* Where did the angel tell Joseph to take Mary and Baby Jesus? *(To Egypt)*

Lesson: Joseph and Mary and Jesus lived in Egypt for a while. Finally, wicked King Herod died. An angel came to Joseph and said, "Joseph, Herod is dead. It is safe to take your family back to the land of Israel."

So Joseph and Mary packed all their things and moved back to the little town of Nazareth. By now, Jesus probably had at least one other brother or sister, but only Jesus was the Son of God. Joseph was the father of the other children. We know that Jesus had four brothers: James, Judah, Joseph and Simeon. We don't know the names of Jesus' sisters. Back in Nazareth, Joseph and Mary made sure their children learned all they would need in life.

Memory Maker: Children in those days studied differently than we do. Little girls had to learn how to cook and make clothes for their families. Their mothers had to buy wool from the shepherds. *(Show white fluff. Let children touch it.)* It was white. So they would fill big pots of hot water and put dye - or color- in the water, then put the wool in the pot to soak. Then they would take the wool out, dry it, and spin it into yarn. *(Show yarn and let children feel it.)* After that, they would weave the yarn on looms to make clothes.

In those days, when boys were six years old, they went to school at the synagogues in their towns. A synagogue is like a church. They learned all about the Old Testament, the first part of our Bibles. They studied until they were twelve. Then they stopped going to school and learned how to do the same kind of work their fathers did.

Jesus went to school, like the other boys. The Bible tells us that Jesus could read and write and that he knew all about God's Word.

In school, one of the most important stories Jesus studied was about Moses, the great leader. For hundreds of years, the Israelites lived in Egypt, where they became slaves of the Pharaohs, Egyptian kings. The Pharaohs made the Israelites build great cities for them

The Egyptians worshipped idols made of stone and wood and gold. But many of the Israelites remembered the one, true God, and they worshipped only him. Their slave masters were cruel, and the Israelites cried out to God to save them from the Egyptians. God heard them and sent Moses to Egypt to rescue them.

At first, the Pharaoh would not let the Israelites leave. But God sent plagues on Egypt until Pharaoh finally let them go. Moses led the Israelites out into the Sinai Desert all the way to a great mountain.

At Mount Sinai, God wrote out laws on tablets of stone. He gave them to Moses to give to the Israelites to teach them how to live in a way that pleased God. These are called the Ten Commandments. In school, Jesus learned about these laws.

The first four of the 10 Commandments were the laws about how we are supposed to show that we love God. This is what they said:

1. I am the Lord your God who rescued you from slavery in Egypt. You shall worship no god except me.

2. You shall not make any idols in the shape of any animal or human or anything else. Do not bow down to idols or worship them.

3. Do not take the name of the Lord your God in vain. That means we should be respectful of God's name.

4. Remember the Sabbath day and keep it holy. You can work six days every week, but not on the seventh day. That is the day to worship God. He wants us to worship him on one special day every week.

The next commandments were about how we are supposed to show love for one another. God told Moses:

5. Honor your father and your mother. That means we are supposed to listen to what they tell us and not disobey them or talk back.

6. You shall not murder.

7. You shall not commit adultery. That means that men and women who are not married to each other are not supposed to live and sleep together the way mommies and daddies do.

8. You shall not steal.

9. You shall not tell lies about your neighbor.

10. You shall not be jealous of anything your neighbor has or want it for yourself.

These were the laws God gave to Moses. Jesus learned these laws very well. All the people in Israel were supposed to obey those same laws.

When Jesus grew older, he told people that all of God's laws were given to us so that we would love God with all our soul-hearts, and that we would love our neighbors in the same way that we love ourselves. Jesus wants each of us to love God and to love one another. Are there other things we can do to show love for God? How can we show love to one another?

Prayer: Dear Father in Heaven, thank you for telling us how to show love to others. Help us to follow your laws so we can make you happy. In Jesus' name, amen.

Chapter 9: John Baptizes Jesus

(What you will need for this lesson: crackers, honey in a bowl; blue cloth or felt and something over which to drape it - like two chairs.)

Review: When Jesus was a boy, did he go to school? *(Yes)* What did Jesus learn? *(He learned about Moses and the 10 Commandments and other Old Testament stories.)* Why did God give us the 10 Commandments? *(To teach us how to love God and others.)* The people in the land of Israel were taught to obey God's laws. Do you think we should obey them, too? *(Yes)*

Lesson: Jesus grew up to be a wonderful man. Because God was his Father, Jesus was not born inside the Sin Trap. Satan tempted him, but Jesus never sinned. He was perfect. Everybody loved him. He was kind and helpful to others. He was a carpenter, like Joseph had been. We don't know when Joseph died, but by the time Jesus was thirty years old, we know that Mary was alone. She was a widow.

It was time for Jesus to start telling people about God and the Rescue Plan. The very first thing he did was to go find his cousin, John, who was six months older than Jesus.

John lived in the desert so he could spend lots of time praying and talking with God. The Bible tells us that he wore clothes made out of camel hair. It was very itchy! He probably wore a thick, leather belt around his waist. The prophet Elijah wore clothes like that, too, and so did lots of other prophets. There wasn't much food out in the desert, so John ate locusts and wild honey. Locusts are like grasshoppers. They are very crunchy.

Memory Maker: *(Serve crackers and honey)* Let's pretend we are visiting John in the desert, and that these crackers are locusts. Let's dip the locusts in honey and eat them!

John loved God with all his heart, and God had a special mission for him. John was supposed to tell people that God wanted them to turn from sin, and to prepare the way for Jesus, the Promised One. Jesus would tell them about the Rescue Plan.

One day John left the desert and went to the Jordan River. It was time for him to start his special job. He began preaching to people there. He said, "Turn away from your sin! Be baptized!"

What did he mean by "baptized"? Back in those days, when a person turned away from something and chose to live in a different way, he showed people he was serious about it by being baptized. That means he went into the water with someone, and that other person dipped him beneath the water for a moment, then lifted him back out of the water.

John was saying that people should get serious about turning away from sin, and show it by being baptized. The Bible tells us that lots and lots of people started coming out to listen to John and to be baptized. People started calling him "John the Baptist."

Then one day while John was baptizing people, Jesus came along. John said, "Look! This is the One who will take away the sins of the world!"

Jesus came down into the water with John. He wanted to be baptized, too. Why? Did Jesus need to turn from sin? No! He never sinned. John said, "Lord! You should baptize me, not have me baptize you!"

But Jesus said, "We need to show people what pleasing God looks like, John. I want everyone who follows me to be baptized, too. In this way they will show other people that they want to stop sinning and to start following God's ways. So baptize me." Jesus did this to set an example for us to follow.

John dipped Jesus under the water. When Jesus came out of the water, the Holy Spirit appeared in the shape of a beautiful white dove and came down on him. Suddenly, a loud voice from heaven said, "This is my beloved Son, in whom I am well pleased!" It was the voice of God!

Jesus was baptized that day to show us what we should do, too. When we give our hearts to Jesus and want to live to please God, Jesus wants us to be baptized, too. That shows our friends and family that we have chosen to follow Jesus. It tells them that we have given our hearts to him and that Jesus lives in our hearts now.

Memory Maker: Let's pretend we are beside the Jordan River with Jesus and John. When we are baptized today, the pastor says, "Upon your confession of faith in Jesus, I now baptize you in the name of the Father and of the Son and of the Holy Spirit." Then he lays us down in the water for a second and brings us back up. It means we have chosen to live for Jesus now. Let's pretend we're being baptized in the Jordan River! *(Drape blue cloth over chairs letting it hang down to the floor on one side. Have one child at a time come around, and you pretend to baptize him, using the words above. To make it more real, tell the child to hold his nose so he won't get water in it while you baptize him.)*

Prayer: Dear Father in Heaven, thank you for taking care of us and loving us. Help us to love and trust you always. Help us show others that we want to follow you. In Jesus' name, amen.

Chapter 10: Fishers Of Men

(What you will need: A big blanket; blue cloth or felt; a fishing pole or stick with string tied to it, and a magnet at the end of the line/string; cut-out hearts with paper clips attached to them.)

Review: In our last story we learned about Jesus and his cousin, John the Baptist. What did John tell people? *(To stop sinning and be baptized)* Why do people get baptized? *(To show that they have turned away from sin and want to follow God.)* Why did Jesus want to be baptized? *(To set an example for us; to show us what we should do.)*

Lesson: Jesus' work on earth had now started. But there was something he needed: disciples. A disciple is someone whom Jesus could teach, who would then teach others.

In the little town of Bethsaida there was a fisherman named Peter. Peter and his brother, Andrew, went out at night on the Sea of Galilee to catch fish to sell the next morning. Their business partners were James and John. Andrew knew about Jesus. He had been at the Jordan River listening to John the Baptist when Jesus had come to be baptized. When Andrew went home, he told Peter, "I have seen the Promised One! His name is Jesus!" Peter, James and John listened with great interest.

Jesus knew all about Peter, Andrew, James and John, because Jesus was the Son of God and he knew all things. He wanted those fishermen to become his disciples. So Jesus went to Bethsaida to see them. When Jesus arrived, he heard that Peter's mother-in-law was sick. So he went to her house. She was in bed with a fever. Jesus told the fever to leave, and it did! The woman got up. She felt great! She said, "Let me fix you a meal!" And she did.

Peter saw this and was very thoughtful when he went to his boat that evening to fish. Fishing was better at night. He and Andrew, James and John climbed into their boats and sailed out into the deep water. They threw their nets into the water then began to haul them back in. But there were no fish in their nets. They fished all night, but could not find a single fish.

Memory Maker: Let's pretend we are fishing with Peter, Andrew, James and John. *(Spread blanket on the floor and shape it like a boat. Step onto the blanket.)* We're going to pretend that this is our boat. Let's throw the net out into the water. Now haul it back in. Oh, no. There aren't any fish! Let's try again! *(Repeat 3 or 4 times.)* That's what Peter, Andrew, James and John did all night long! It took a lot of energy. But by morning, they had still not caught even one fish. They rowed to shore, tired and ready to go to bed. Let's get out of our boat and go back to our seats now.

There was a crowd of people on the shore. "Where's Jesus?" someone shouted to the fishermen in the boat.

"We don't know!" Peter shouted back. He and Andrew pulled their boat out of the water. A little while later, Peter saw Jesus off in a quiet place, away from the lake. "Teacher," he said, "people are looking for you out on the beach."

So Jesus went out to the beach to teach the people about God and to heal those who were sick. Even though he was tired, Peter stayed to hear what Jesus had to say. Jesus climbed into Peter's boat and preached from there. After he finished teaching, Jesus said, "Peter, let's go out into the water a ways."

Peter and Andrew took their boat out a little ways. "Peter," Jesus said, "throw your net into the water."

Peter was tired. He said, "Master, we have fished all night and have caught nothing! But because you ask, I will do it." He sighed and grabbed the net. He threw it out into the water.

Suddenly, the net was filled with fish! He held on and pulled. "Andrew! Come help!" Peter yelled. Andrew grabbed at the net. "It's too full!" Peter yelled toward the shore, "James! John! Help us!"

James and John quickly pushed their boat into the water and sailed out to Peter and Andrew. Together, they hauled the net full of fish into the boat. It was so full that it almost broke!

When the tired fishermen reached the shore, Jesus stepped out of Peter's boat and smiled. "Follow me, and I will make you fishers of men!"

What did Jesus mean by that? Did he mean that those who follow him would go around pulling people out of water? No! He meant that everyone who follows him should tell others about Jesus, and about how God wants us to live. Then they might want to follow Jesus, too.

So Peter, Andrew, James and John left their nets and boats and followed Jesus. Two other men from Bethsaida went with them as well: Philip and his friend, Nathaniel. Six more disciples soon joined them. Their names were Matthew, Judas, Thaddeus, Thomas, Simon, and another man named James. Twelve men followed Jesus and learned about God from him.

As these men learned about Jesus, the Son of God, they began helping other people to trust in Jesus, too. Soon lots and lots of people followed Jesus! This is what Jesus meant when he told the disciples to become fishers of men. But not just men! Jesus wants women and children, too. He wants us all to be fishers of people! How can we do that?

Memory Maker: *(Put a piece of blue cloth/felt in the shape of a pond on the floor. Put red paper hearts on it. Bring out fishing poles.)* We are going to practice being fishers of people today. This is our pretend pond with hearts in it. We are going to pretend that these hearts belong to people who don't know about Jesus. When I give you a fishing pole, hold it over the hearts and say, "Jesus loves you!" Then catch a heart with your fishing pole and bring it out of the water. Telling people that Jesus loves them is something even children can do! *(Let each child catch 2 or 3 hearts.)*

Prayer: Dear Father in Heaven, thank you for sending Jesus to bless us and to help us become fishers of men and women and boys and girls! Help us to tell our friends about your Son, Jesus, so they can give their hearts to him and get out of the Sin Trap. In Jesus' name, amen.

Chapter 11: The Sermon on the Mount, Part 1

(What you will need: Sin Trap; Cut out large paper hearts in many colors - at least 8 hearts - and make sure you have one heart for each child in class. You will need putty or tape for children to put hearts on wall. Draw a smile on the front of each heart. Each time you give a heart to a child, pause and have him put it on the wall.)

Review: When God first made the world, everything was perfect and beautiful. Was there any pain or sadness or anything bad in it? *(No!)* But after Adam and Eve sinned, people's hearts were caught in what? *(show the Sin Trap)* Satan became the ruler of this world. He caused many bad things: sickness, wars, mean people, and death. People's hearts were sad.

Lesson: But now Jesus was on earth. He told people that if they would trust and obey God again, God would watch over them and give them happy hearts. People came from everywhere to listen to Jesus. They brought sick children to Jesus and he healed them.

One day, they came to where Jesus was walking on a mountain. When Jesus saw them, he sat down in a place where everyone could hear him, and he began to teach. We are going to pretend we are sitting on the mountainside with Jesus today, and listen to what he said. Jesus told people:

(Show a heart) God gives happy hearts to those who feel they are not important. He gives them the kingdom of heaven! When we give Jesus our love, our trust and our heart, then God makes us his own children! Yes, we still belong to our earthly parents, too. God is the great King over everything. What do you call a child of a king? A prince or princess! That is what we become, in God's eyes! Does that make our hearts happy? Yes! *(Give a heart to a child. Have child put heart on wall.)* When we don't feel important, remember that we are important to God, and he wants to give us happy hearts!

(Show another heart, give to child.) God gives happy hearts to those who are sad. He comforts them! When our hearts are sad, we can tell God about it, and he will wrap his arms around us and make us feel better. Whenever we are sad, remember that God wants to give us happy hearts!

(Show another heart, give to child.) God gives happy hearts to those who are gentle and poor. He gives them the whole world! Right now we may not have much. Sometimes people may take things away from us. We might not have warm clothes or enough food or other important things. Whenever we need something, we can ask God to help us. He always listens, and he wants to help us and to give us happy hearts!

(Show another heart, give to a child) God gives happy hearts to those who are hungry and thirsty for God's ways. He fills them up! When we want to be like Jesus, when we want to see people treated fairly, when we want to see people living to please God, that means we are hungry and thirsty for God's ways. God wants to fill us up with Jesus and give us happy hearts!

(Show a heart, give to a child) God gives happy hearts to those who are merciful. He shows them mercy! What is mercy? If someone has done something wrong and they are going to be punished, but then someone forgives them and lets them go free, that is mercy. God will forgive us when we forgive others. When we forgive others, God gives us happy hearts!

(Show a heart, give to a child) God gives happy hearts to those whose hearts are pure. They will see his face! What does it mean to have a pure heart? It means we want to think only good things that please God. We cannot do that by ourselves, but Jesus can help us to have pure hearts. God gives us happy hearts when our hearts are pure. We can know that someday we will see God's face!

(Show a heart, give to a child) God gives happy hearts to those who try to make peace. He calls them his own children! There are lots of people in this world who fight. When we try to make peace, God calls us his own children. When we help others to treat each other nicely, God gives us happy hearts!

(Show a heart, give to a child) God gives happy hearts to those who are teased and treated badly because they live for Jesus. He gives them the kingdom of heaven! Has anyone ever teased you or made fun of you because you are a Christian? Jesus said that someday you will be in heaven, and that's a terrific reward! If others tease us about Jesus, always remember that God will give us happy hearts because he loves us so much!

(Make sure each child has a heart to put on the wall.) Does Jesus give happy hearts to everyone who will trust and obey him? Yes! He loves us so much! And he wants to give each one of US a happy heart!

One day when Jesus was teaching, some mothers brought their children to him. They wanted Jesus to bless their children. But Jesus' disciples told the mothers, "Jesus is too busy to talk to you and your children. Go away!"

But Jesus was upset when he heard that! He said, "No! Do not send them away! Let the little children come to me! Don't stop them! The kingdom of heaven is made of little ones just like these!" So the children went to Jesus and he blessed them.

Memory Maker: What does it mean to bless someone? I want all of you to come up here by me now. Sit on the floor, and I will bless you like Jesus blessed the children, so you will know what it is like. *(Put your hands on each child's head as you bless him. Look the child straight in the eye. Sample blessings: "God has given you special abilities. May God watch over you every day and help you to use your special abilities for him; May you always live to please God." Or you can compare the children to animals or things God has created: "You are like a lion. You are strong in Jesus and stand up for him. May God keep you strong for Jesus all your life." You can make a list of each child's qualities in advance and ask God to give you wise words for each child.)*

Prayer: Dear Father in Heaven, Thank you that you promise to give us all happy hearts when we trust and obey you. Help us to remember this when we are sad. In Jesus' name, amen.

Chapter 12: Sermon On The Mount, Part 2

(What you will need: a large, colorful, cut-out heart; mustard seeds; bread & fish — which can be tuna in small cups or goldfish crackers; paper napkins or wash cloth if using tuna; two baskets for bread and fish)

Review: When Jesus started teaching people about God, what was the first thing he told them? *(Hold up a smiling heart. Let the children try to remember.)* God gives happy hearts to those who trust and obey him. Do you think people wanted to hear more about God because of what Jesus said? *(Yes!)* Today we are going to hear more things Jesus said about his Father, God.

Lesson: Jesus had more to say about God the Father. He told people, "Don't worry about whether you will have enough to eat, or what you will wear. Look at the birds! They don't need to plant or gather food into barns! But your heavenly Father feeds them. And YOU are much more valuable to him than the birds are!"

"And why worry about your clothes?" Jesus said. "Look at the flowers in the fields. They don't even work or make their own clothes. Yet King Solomon in all his beautiful clothes was not prettier than these flowers. If God clothes the flowers of the field -flowers that are here one day and gone the next - don't you think he will take care of you?"

Jesus told people that when we trust God -- when we have faith -- all things are possible. He said, "If you have faith the size of a mustard seed, you can say to a mountain, 'Be moved!' And the mountain will fall into the sea!"

Memory Maker: Do you know how big a mustard seed is? *(Show mustard seeds - let children handle them.)* It isn't very big at all! Jesus said that even if our faith is very small, we can still do great things for him. We can ask God for anything, in Jesus' name, and if it is good for us, God will do it. If someone is sick, we can ask God to make that person well again. If we need food, we can ask God to help us, and he will. If we are afraid, we can ask God the Father to make us not be afraid. God will always hear us and help us if we have faith!

One day when Jesus finished teaching, he looked around at all the people. Five thousand men and their families had followed him to learn about God! He thought, "These people have been listening to me all day! They are hungry!" So Jesus asked his disciples, "Where can we get food to feed all these people?"

The disciples were very upset! They told Jesus, "It would take all the money we could make in a year! We couldn't ever save up enough money to feed that many people!"

But Jesus smiled. What had he just told everyone? Trust GOD to feed us! Do you think Jesus had a plan to feed the people? Yes! And do you know who was going to help him with his big plan?

It was not a grown-up who would help Jesus! One of the disciples -- Andrew -- went out into the crowd and started looking for food. He came back to Jesus leading a boy. "Jesus," he said, "here is a boy with five barley loaves and two small fish. But what are these among so many?"

Jesus looked at the boy and smiled. The boy handed Jesus his lunch. Jesus thanked his Father, God, for the food the boy had brought. Then he began to break the bread and fish. He handed it to the disciples. Every time Jesus broke off a piece of bread or fish, more bread and fish appeared in the basket! The disciples took baskets of food to everyone in the crowd. All the people on the mountain with Jesus were fed!

Memory Maker: Let's pretend we are out on that mountain with Jesus. *(Have 2 children hold baskets, one of bread and one of fish- or fish crackers.)* Jesus took the bread and fish and thanked God for it. Let's do that. Thank you, Father God, for giving us food to eat. Amen. Then Jesus broke the food into pieces and gave it to the crowd. *(Break bread and have helpers pass it and the fish around. Eat together.)*

Afterward, Jesus said, "Now I want you to gather up what is left." The disciples collected the leftovers. Do you know how much food was left? Twelve baskets full!

So you see, when we follow Jesus and have faith in him, we can trust him to take care of all our needs.

Prayer: Dear Father in Heaven, help us to follow Jesus in all we do and say. Help us to trust and obey you always. In Jesus' name, amen.

Chapter 13: The Grateful Leper

(What you will need: paper and pencil or crayons)

Review: Jesus told us that we should not worry about clothes or food, because God would give us those things when we trust and obey him. Then Jesus told his disciples to feed a big, big crowd of people. But the disciples couldn't think of a way to do it. Who helped Jesus feed the people? *(a little boy)* What did the little boy give Jesus? *(his lunch - 5 loaves and 2 fish)* Jesus showed us how God can take care of everything we need.

Lesson: Today we are going to learn about a man who had a very big need. In a small town on the edge of Israel there lived a man and his family. They were happy together and loved each other very much. But one day the man noticed a white spot on his hand. He rubbed it, hoping it would go away. But it didn't. The next day the spot was bigger.

The man was afraid! In those days, there was a bad disease called leprosy. It started with a small white spot on the skin. Then the spot would get larger and more spots would grow. The spots would cause fingers and toes to fall off! Anyone who had leprosy had to leave the town so nobody else would get the disease from him.

When his family came together, the man showed them the white spot on his hand. "I will have to show this to the priest," he said. "If the priest tells me it is leprosy, I will have to leave you so that you won't get this, too."

Everyone in the man's family was sad. The wife didn't want her husband to leave! The children didn't want to have to say good-bye to their daddy! When the priest saw the spot, he said, "I'm sorry, friend, but this is leprosy. You will have to leave town."

The man's heart was very sad. He took some clothes and blankets and food and went away from his home. He went out into the hills near the town where other lepers lived. There may have been a cave to live in, or a shelter of some kind. There were nine lepers living together, and the man joined them. Now there were ten.

All the lepers were sad. As the leprosy spread to their faces, they put cloths over them to hide the sores. When the leprosy spread to their fingers, they wrapped the fingers to protect them from cold. Slowly, the leprosy ate away at their bodies. Some could not walk because the leprosy made their toes fall off.

Every day, the lepers' families would bring food out to them. The families had to stay away and could not come close. The man's wife and children brought food to him, too. When he saw his family, the man would wave sadly and call out, "I love you!" And his family would call, "We love you, too!"

One day someone called out to the lepers, "Jesus is coming to town!" Some of the lepers were very excited. They knew about Jesus!

"Who is Jesus?" the man asked.

Another leper said, "Jesus is the Promised One! He teaches about God, and he heals people!"

"Do you think he would heal us?" the leper asked.

"We can ask him!" someone said. "Yes! let's do that!"

So the next day when Jesus and his disciples were coming into town, the ten lepers ran out toward the road and called to him. "Jesus! Jesus! Please heal us!"

Jesus went up to them and looked into their faces. He wasn't afraid of leprosy! He smiled. "Go show yourselves to the priest," he said.

The lepers were excited! This meant Jesus had healed them! Without waiting, they turned and began running toward town to see the priest.

The man reached up to feel his face. His face was healed! He took off the bandages on his hands. His hands were well! His fingers were okay! Jesus had healed him! The man's heart was full of love for Jesus. He stopped running and turned back.

The man ran to Jesus and looked up into his face. "Praise God!" he said. "I am healed!" The man knelt down in front of Jesus and said, "Oh, thank you, Jesus! Thank you! Now I can go home to my family! I can hug my wife and children again! Thank you!"

Jesus smiled at the man. Then he looked up and saw the other lepers running toward town and grew sad. "I healed ten. Where are the other nine?" he asked.

The leper shook his head in amazement. Why hadn't the other lepers thanked Jesus? He did not know. He stood up and thanked Jesus again, then he ran home to his family. Jesus had made his heart happy again.

Jesus still does many things for people today. When we pray and ask Jesus to help us, he does. When we need things, we ask Jesus for those things, and he makes sure we have everything we need. Isn't Jesus wonderful?

Yes, he is. But what about us? Are we like the nine who ran to town and didn't say thank you? Or are we like the one who did say thank you? When Jesus helps us and gives us happy hearts, we need to remember to say "thank you" to him. That makes Jesus' heart happy!

Memory Maker: Let's make a list of some things for which we want to thank Jesus. (*Have children tell of things Jesus has done for them — make a list on a whiteboard or on a piece of paper. Put the list in a place where you can see it.*) Let's thank God now!

Prayer: Dear Father in Heaven, thank you for all these wonderful things you have done for us! Help us to remember to say "thank you" every day. In Jesus' name, amen.

Chapter 14: Jesus And Peter Walk On Water

(What you will need: a blanket; 2-3 pillows; fish-shaped crackers or tuna; juice or water; napkins or washcloth for clean-up, if you use tuna)

Review: We have learned that Jesus fed large crowds of people. He made sick people well. He taught us how much God loves us and that he wants to give us happy hearts.

Lesson: But one day Jesus was very sad. Do you remember the bad King Herod who had tried to kill Jesus when he was a baby? That King Herod had died, but his son was now the king. His name was Herod, too, and he was bad. Jesus was sad because some friends of his cousin, John the Baptist, came to him with a message. Bad King Herod had killed John!

Jesus wanted to be alone to cry and to talk to his heavenly Father. So he and his disciples got into their boat and sailed away to a far place. But the crowds of people who wanted to see Jesus followed them. They brought their sick people for Jesus to heal. When Jesus saw them, he was sorry for them and he spent all day healing the sick and telling people about God the Father. That was the same day Jesus fed over five thousand people with only five barley loaves and two small fish from a boy's lunch. Jesus helped people even when he was sad.

By the end of the day when everyone had gone home, Jesus was very tired. He still needed to be alone to talk to his heavenly Father and to cry because John was dead. So he sent the disciples away in the boat then went up into the hills to pray.

Late that night, a strong wind began to blow. Jesus knew what that meant! The wind would make great big waves on the Sea of Galilee, where his disciples were. He knew they were in trouble!

Out on the Sea of Galilee, the disciples were battling the big waves. Water splashed into the boat! They bailed it out. They cried out, "God! Save us from this storm!"

Just then, one of the disciples looked up. He saw someone walking on the water! "A ghost!" he yelled. The others looked up and saw the person, too. "Oh, no!" they cried in fear.

But then they heard a voice call to them. "Don't be afraid! It is I, Jesus!"

What? Jesus was walking on the water? Wow! It couldn't be true!

Peter shouted, "Lord, if that is you, command me to come to you on the water!"

Jesus smiled. "Yes, Peter. Come!"

So Peter stood up bravely and stepped out of the boat onto the water. And he didn't sink! He took a step, then another and another. Yes! He was walking on water! He was almost to Jesus.

The other disciples watched. Their eyes got very big.

Suddenly, Peter saw a big wave rising up in the water, and he was terrified! He took his eyes off Jesus and watched the wave. Then he began to sink! Oh, no! "Jesus! Lord! Save me!" Peter cried.

Jesus reached out and grabbed Peter. He smiled. "Where is your faith, Peter? Why did you doubt?" he said, pulling him out of the water.

Peter was not afraid anymore. Jesus was with him! Together, they walked across the water to the boat and climbed into it.

Immediately, the wind and waves stopped, and the boat settled down. Jesus had saved them again. The disciples worshipped Jesus and said, "Jesus, you truly are the Son of God!"

Jesus said Peter did not have much faith. What does "faith" mean? It means we believe God. Do you think Peter had more faith than the other disciples? He was the only one who stepped out of the boat and walked on water with Jesus! I think he had more faith! His faith only left him when he took his eyes off Jesus. But Jesus gave Peter a second chance to show that he had faith. He helped Peter out of the water and walked to the boat with him.

We may not always have enough faith to be strong for Jesus, but Jesus will always give us more chances to learn faith. He wants us to do great things for God! Do you want to grow strong in faith? I do!

Memory Maker: (*Spread blanket on floor in shape of a boat. Lay pillows lengthwise, end-to-end, across floor.*) Let's pretend we are in the boat with the disciples. This will be our pretend boat. (*Everyone get into the "boat".*) The storm is tossing the boat around. Let's pretend the boat is rocking! (*Move from side to side like you are on the water.*) Oh, look! There's Jesus! He's walking on the water! What is he saying? He's saying, "Peter, get out of the boat and come walk with me!" Who wants to be Peter? (*One child at a time can be Peter.*) Okay - I'll go stand where Jesus is, and I will say "Come to me!" Then you get out of the boat and walk on the water toward me. When you are almost there, pretend to fall into the water and cry, "Lord, save me!" (*Have child walk on pillows. When child "falls" and calls out, say, "Where's your faith? Why did you doubt." Help the child up and walk with him to the boat. After everyone is finished, say . . .*) Ok. We're at the shore. Let's get out of the boat and fix breakfast. Let's build a pretend fire and cook our food. (*Food will be fish-shaped crackers --or tuna in little cups or plates– and juice or water.*)

Before we eat, let's talk to God about learning to grow in faith.

Prayer: Dear Father in Heaven, help me to learn to trust you more every day. Make my faith grow so I can do great things for you! In Jesus' name, amen.

Chapter 15: Jairus' Daughter

(What you will need: a paper and pen/pencil)

Review: Jesus taught us to trust God for all things, not just our food and clothes, but also for making us well when we are sick. Is it important to thank God for the things he does for us? *(Yes)* We learned about faith, too. What is faith? *(Faith means we believe God.)* Peter believed God and he walked on water!

Lesson: Our Bible story today is about a man named Jairus. Jairus was the worship leader at the temple in his town. He had a wife and a little girl, whom he loved so much. One day the little girl got sick. As the days passed, she got worse and worse, until finally Jairus knew she was dying. His heart was breaking! "What can I do to save her?" he wondered. Then he thought about Jesus! Jesus was visiting his town! Jesus could heal his little girl! So he left the house and went out looking for Jesus.

But there were no phones back then, and no televisions or radios. So Jairus didn't know where Jesus was. He started asking people, "Do you know where Jesus is?" Finally, someone told him, "I saw Jesus talking to a big crowd of people." He told Jairus how to find Jesus.

Jairus ran toward Jesus as fast as he could. There was a huge crowd of people around Jesus. "Let me through! Let me through!" Jairus begged.

Everyone knew Jairus because he was their worship leader. "Let him through!" they began calling out.

Jairus finally broke through the crowd to where Jesus was teaching. "Master!" he cried. He fell down on his knees before Jesus. "My little girl is sick. I think she is dying! Won't you please come to my house and heal her?"

Jesus looked at Jairus and said, "Yes, I will." Jesus turned to his disciples and said, "You stay here and teach people about God, all except for Peter, James and John. You three come with me."

Just then a man pushed through the crowd to Jairus. "It's too late, Jairus," he said. "Your little girl just died. It's too late for Jesus to help."

Jairus' heart broke. He began to cry. Not his little girl!

But Jesus said, "Jairus, it's not too late. Let's go to your house." Jairus turned and started leading Jesus out of the crowd.

But there was a sick lady in the crowd who needed to see Jesus, too. She had been sick for twelve years! She had seen a lot of doctors, but nobody could heal her. It had been hard for her to walk all the way to Jesus, but she knew that if she could just touch his robe, she would be healed. "Oh, no!" she thought when she heard Jesus say he would go with Jairus. "Not now! I came all this way!"

Jairus was leading Jesus through the crowd. They were coming her way. Maybe, just maybe Jesus would get close enough, the woman thought.

Sure enough, he did. He walked right by her! The woman reached out and touched the edge of Jesus' robe. Suddenly, she felt well all over!

Jesus stopped. "Who touched me?" he asked.

"What do you mean?" his disciples asked. "There are lots of people who touched you!"

"I felt healing power go out of me," Jesus said. "Someone touched me."

The very shy woman stepped forward. "I touched you, Master," she said. "I have been sick for twelve years. I have spent all my money on doctors, but nobody has been able to heal me. Just now I touched your robe, and now I am well!" Her face was so happy.

Jesus looked at her and said, "Daughter, your faith has made you well. Go in peace." Wow! The woman had faith in Jesus. She had only touched his robe, and Jesus had healed her!

When Jairus saw what Jesus had done, do you think he began to have faith, too? Yes! He knew that woman. He knew she had been sick for many years. If Jesus could heal her, maybe Jesus could help his little girl.

Jesus said, "Don't worry, Jairus. Just trust me, and your little girl will be well again."

Together, Jairus and Jesus went to the house. There were people gathered around it, crying loudly because the little girl had died.

Jesus said, "Stop crying. The little girl is not dead. She is only sleeping." But the people laughed at Jesus. They knew the child was dead.

Jesus took Peter, James and John into the house with him, along with Jairus and his wife. He went over to the little girl and reached down and took her hand. "Little girl, arise!" Jesus said.

The little girl opened her eyes, took a deep breath and sat up! She was alive! Jesus had raised her from the dead.

Jairus' heart was so happy! "Thank you, Jesus! Thank you!" he said.

The little girl's mother was so excited. Jesus had raised their little girl from the dead! It was a great miracle.

Jesus laughed with joy to see Jairus so happy.

The Bible tells us that Jesus is the same today as he was then. Just like Jairus, when you need Jesus to help you with something, all you need to do is ask him and Jesus will help you.

Will Jesus always do exactly what you ask? Not always. Sometimes his answer will be different than we expect. But Jesus wants us to always ask him for what we need and trust that he will always give us the best answer of all. That is how we show faith in him. It is how we learn to trust him.

Memory Maker: Are there things you want to ask God for today? Let's make a list and pray about them now. Remember that we should always ask in Jesus' name. *(Write a list of prayer requests then pray for God to answer them.)* Let's keep this list in our Bible and check it often to see what God's answer is.

Prayer: Dear Father in Heaven, here are the things we need from you. Please answer our prayers in the way you think is best. We trust you! In Jesus' name, amen.

Chapter 16: Jesus Visits Friends

(What you will need: cookies or fruit; Bible; a pencil & paper)

Review: In our last lesson, we heard about a man named Jairus and about his little girl. Do you remember what happened? *(Jairus' daughter got sick and died. Jairus trusted Jesus, and Jesus raised the little girl from the dead.)* That shows us how powerful Jesus is!

Lesson: Today we are going to learn something about what Jesus wants us to do for him. Martha and her sister Mary lived in the little town of Bethany with their brother, Lazarus. Jesus was one of their best friends.

One day, Jesus told his disciples, "Let's go visit Martha, Mary and Lazarus."

When Jesus and his twelve disciples came to Martha's house, Martha was very excited. "Come in! Come in, Jesus!" she said. "Come in, friends!"

Mary and Lazarus welcomed them, too. "Come sit down!" they said.

Visitors from the village saw that Jesus was at Martha's house, and some of them came to the house, too. "Tell us about God!" they said to Jesus.

So Jesus began to talk about his heavenly Father. Mary sat down near Jesus' feet and listened. She wanted to hear every word Jesus said.

But Martha saw all the people there and started wondering how to feed Jesus and his disciples and all the other people. She went to her storeroom and brought out jars of dried fruit and maybe even some small sweets. "Jesus will like this!" she thought. Maybe she took a basket of food into the room and passed it around.

> **Memory Maker:** *(Pass food around to children and eat together.)* Oh, yes. The food is very good. Do you think Jesus liked Martha's food? Yes!

Martha probably thought, "I'll have to do a lot of cooking to feed everyone, too. Hm. Shall I do a big barbecue? Let's see. I'll need to roast a lamb. Will that be enough food? No! I'll have to bake bread, too. Mary only mixed up enough bread for our own family. I'll have to get her to help me. Where is she?"

Martha hurried into the room where Jesus was talking. "Jesus," she said, "please send Mary out here to help me!"

But Jesus said, "Martha, Martha. You are so worried about lots of little things that don't matter. But Mary has chosen what is best, and it shall not be taken away from her."

What did Jesus mean? Wasn't food important? Yes, food was important. But remember how Jesus fed five-thousand people with only five barley loaves and two small fish? Jesus could make the food himself!

Do you think Martha went back to fixing food? Or did she come in and sit down with Mary? I think she came into the room and sat down with the others and listened to Jesus.

Jesus told them what he had been telling the large crowds of people. "God loves you! He watches over you. You don't need to worry about food. When you follow God and bring other people to him, God will feed you, too." So, "Don't store up treasures on earth. If you do, moths will eat the cloth and the metal things will rust. Thieves can break into your house and steal your treasure. But if you store up treasure in Heaven, you will have treasure forever!"

How do we store up treasure in heaven?

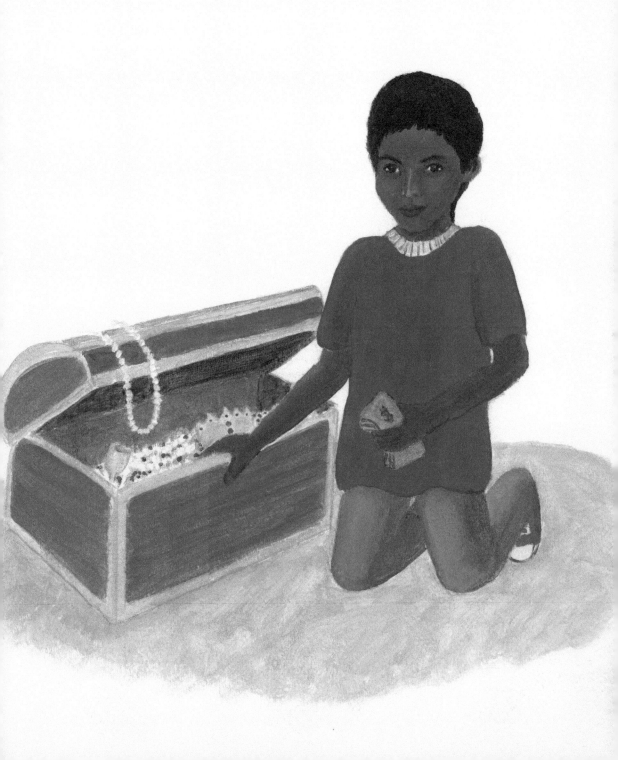

If we see others who are sad, we should comfort them. If others are sick, how can we help them? Can we bring them food or help with their work? If someone doesn't have a place to live, how can we help him? We can share our home with him. If people don't have enough clothes to keep warm, how can we help them? We can share some of our clothes. This shows them that God loves them, too.

Jesus said that when we help others, it is the same as helping him! That is how we store up treasures in heaven. Someday, when Jesus comes back to earth, God the Father will reward us for all we have done for Jesus.

Mary, Martha and Lazarus listened closely to what Jesus taught them. But Mary listened best of all. Jesus wants us to listen to him like that!

How can we listen to Jesus like Mary did? God had his prophets and disciples write down what he wants us to know. We have those words in our Bible.

Memory Maker: *(Hold up Bible.)* The Bible is like a love letter from God. When we read the Bible *(open Bible)* we hear God's words to us. When we pray, we talk with God. If we read our Bibles and pray to God every day, we can be like Mary, too. When we listen to God, he makes our hearts happy. We make God's heart happy when we talk to him. What would you like to tell God? *(As children tell you what they want God to know, write it down. Fold it and put it in an envelope. On the outside write: To God.)* Let's put this in our Bible, God's special Book.

Prayer: Dear Father in Heaven, thank you for loving us and wanting us to talk with you. Thank you for giving us the Bible so we can listen to you, like Mary did. In Jesus' name, amen.

Chapter 17: Jesus Calms Storm And Casts Out Demons

(What you will need: a large blanket)

Review: Jesus and his disciples traveled all around the Sea of Galilee, and Jesus would teach people in every place their boat landed. He would heal the sick, too. And he even raised a little girl from the dead! *(Jairus' daughter)*

Lesson: One day, Jesus was very tired. When he got into the boat to go to the next town with his disciples, he fell asleep. While Jesus was sleeping, a terrible storm arose. Have you ever seen a big lake or the ocean during a storm? It can be scary! That was how it was on the Sea of Galilee that day. The wind blew! The waves grew bigger and bigger! The disciples were very afraid!

Memory Maker: Let's pretend we are in that boat with the disciples. *(Spread blanket on floor, folding ends to make it look like a boat. Have children sit in "boat".)* Can you imagine the waves? Let's pretend the waves are rocking the boat around. Oh, no! The waves are splashing into the boat! Let's bail the water out! Here comes a bigger wave! Somebody wake Jesus up! The disciples cried out, "Jesus! Wake up!" Let's say that together: "Jesus! Wake up!"

Jesus awoke. He saw the storm. He saw how afraid his disciples were. Then Jesus rose up. He held out his hands and told the wind and waves, "Peace! Be still!" And do you know what? The storm stopped RIGHT NOW! The disciples looked at each other in surprise. "Who is this? Even the wind and the waves obey him!"

When the boat reached the shore, they were near a town. They climbed out of the boat and tied it up. Let's all climb out of the boat and go back to our seats now.

Jesus and his disciples climbed the hill next to the seashore. High up on the hill, there were graves in the cliffs. People used to bury the dead in caves. A man was wandering around the graves. There were broken chains on his arms and legs from when people had tried to chain him up. He was moaning and crying out. He had no clothes. He was wild and dangerous. When the man saw Jesus, he rushed up to him and said, "Leave us alone! What have we to do with you, Son of God?"

Why did he say, "Leave us alone?" It was because some demons - Satan's bad angels - were inside his body. Can demons get inside people who belong to Jesus? No! Because Jesus lives in their hearts. Satan and his bad angles cannot go where Jesus is. But this man didn't know about Jesus yet.

Jesus said, "What is your name?"

The demons in the man cried out, "Legion!" That means many thousands. The poor man had many thousands of demons living in his body! No wonder he was wild and dangerous!

Jesus saw that the man was filled with demons and felt sorry for him. Jesus is stronger than all the demons because he is the Son of God. He has all the power! The demons know it. That day, they begged Jesus, "Please! If you are going to cast us out of this man, let us go into that herd of pigs over there so we can still have bodies to live in!"

Jesus gave them permission and said, "Go!"

The demons rushed out of the man and into the pigs. All the pigs started squealing and bucking and running! They were so upset that they ran right off a cliff into the sea and drowned!

But the wild man was safe now that the demons were gone. He was very tired, and the disciples put some clothes on him.

The men whose job it was to watch the pigs ran back to the town and told everyone what had happened. Do you think those people were happy Jesus had cast the demons out of that man?

They were all very surprised! They went out to Jesus. They saw the man Jesus had saved from the demons. He was dressed and sitting quietly on a rock. But all their pigs were gone! The people weren't happy at all. They were afraid of Jesus! They begged him, "Please leave us alone!"

Isn't that strange? They were so afraid of Jesus' power that they wanted him to leave! But the man Jesus had saved wanted to go with him. "Please!" he begged. "Let me follow you, Jesus!"

But Jesus told him, "No, I need you to stay in this town and tell everyone what great things God has done for you." Why did Jesus say that? Jesus wanted the man to tell the people about him so they would believe and be rescued from the Sin Trap, too. That's why the man needed to stay in his town.

Is Jesus the Boss of the wind and the waves? Yes! Is Jesus the Boss of demons? Yes! Is Jesus more powerful than death? Yes! Remember, he raised a little girl from the dead. Jesus is the Boss of everything! When Jesus is the Boss, good things happen. Do you want Jesus to be the Boss of you?

Prayer: Dear Jesus, I love you so much! I want you to be the Boss of me and help me to tell others all about you. In your name we pray, amen.

Chapter 18: Jesus Raises Lazarus

(What you will need: white cloth or a sheet to wrap around a child like a mummy)

Review: Do you remember Jesus' friends, Mary, Martha and Lazarus? They lived in a little town called Bethany, very close to Jerusalem. Lazarus and Jesus were very good friends. Do you remember how Martha worked hard trying to get food ready for Jesus? But what did Mary do? *(She sat at Jesus' feet and listened to him.)*

Lesson: One day, Lazarus became sick. Soon he was so sick he couldn't leave his bed. Martha and Mary tried everything they could to make him well, but Lazarus did not get any better.

"We need Jesus to heal Lazarus!" Martha said. She called in a friend and told him, "Please go up into Galilee and find Jesus for us! Tell him that Lazarus is very sick and we need Jesus to heal him. Go as fast as you can! Lazarus is very, very sick!"

The messenger left and traveled quickly to the Sea of Galilee where Jesus was healing people and teaching. When the messenger found Jesus, he said, "Master! Lazarus, the one you love, is sick!"

But Jesus told him, "This sickness will not end in death, but will show the glory of God. People will know that I am the Promised One because of this sickness."

So the messenger left. When he reached Mary and Martha, he told them what Jesus said. But they were not comforted. Lazarus had died!

Mary and Martha were so sad.

Memory Maker: Mary and Martha wrapped Lazarus up, getting him ready to put in the tomb. Would someone like to pretend to be Lazarus? *(Choose volunteer.)* This is how Mary and Martha wrapped Lazarus. *(Wrap child in white cloth, except for his face.)* Okay. That is how Lazarus was wrapped. Now let's unwrap you. *(Unwrap child and send him back to his seat.)*

In Galilee, Jesus told his disciples, "It is time to go to see Mary and Martha now."

"But Jesus!" the disciples said, "The religious leaders in Jerusalem don't like you, and last time we were there, they tried to kill you! We shouldn't go back there!"

Jesus said, "We must go. Our friend, Lazarus, has fallen asleep. I must go awaken him."

The disciples said, "Oh. If he is sleeping, then he will get well."

"No," Jesus said, "Lazarus is dead. I am going to him now."

When Jesus and his disciples arrived at Martha's house, there was a great crowd of friends who had come to comfort them. Martha saw Jesus and went out to meet him. She was crying. She went up to him and said, "Lord, if you had just been here, Lazarus would not have died! Even now, I know that whatever you ask God, he will give it to you."

Jesus said, "Yes, Martha. Lazarus will rise from the dead."

Martha said, "I know he will. . . someday, when God raises all people from the dead."

Jesus said, "Martha, **I AM** the resurrection and the life! Whoever believes in me will live, even if he dies. Anyone who believes in me will never really die. Do you believe this, Martha?"

Martha looked up at Jesus and said, "Yes, Lord. I believe. You are the Promised One, the Son of God."

"Where is Mary?" Jesus asked.

Martha left Jesus standing there and went to find her sister. "Mary," she said, "Jesus is here. He's asking for you."

Mary wiped the tears from her eyes and went out to see Jesus. She knelt at his feet and said, "Lord, if you had been here, Lazarus would not have died!"

Tears came to Jesus' eyes. "Mary, where did you put Lazarus?" Mary and Martha led Jesus to the grave in the side of the hill where they had put Lazarus' body.

Jesus said, "Roll the stone away."

"But Jesus!" Martha protested. "Lazarus has been dead four days now! His body smells bad!"

Jesus said, "Didn't I tell you that if you believe in me, you will see something very special from God the Father?"

So Martha had some men roll the gravestone away. The crowd came near. What was Jesus going to do? They knew he had raised a few people from the dead. But all those people had been dead only a short time. Lazarus was very, very dead! Four days dead!

Jesus stood in front of the grave and called in a loud voice, "Lazarus! Come forth!" Everyone held their breath and stared into the dark grave. Suddenly, they saw something moving! It was Lazarus! He was all wrapped up in grave clothes, but he was walking out of the grave!

Jesus smiled at Lazarus, and Lazarus smiled back. Jesus told the people, "Unwrap those grave clothes so he can walk!" Mary and Martha and their friends started to unwrap Lazarus. Someone ran back to the house and brought some clothes for him. Lazarus was alive! Everyone was excited. Many who were there believed in Jesus that day.

Because Adam and Eve sinned, all people will someday die. Our bodies wear out and fail. The soul-hearts of everyone who believes in Jesus will go to heaven to be with him when their bodies die. But when Jesus comes back to earth, he will raise to life all the bodies of everyone who believes in him.

Memory Maker: *(Use a strong, commanding voice. Look each child in the eye and point at him when you say, "Come forth!")* Jesus will call your name and say, "*(Child's name)*, come forth!" *(Do this with each child.)* And when Jesus calls, you **will** come out of the grave, because **Jesus** is the Resurrection and the Life. Everyone who believes in him will live again, even though he has died. Jesus will give us new bodies, ones that will never die. Then we will be filled with joy and live with him forever and ever!

Prayer: Dear Father in heaven, thank you for sending Jesus to give us life! We believe that Jesus will raise us all from the dead when he comes back to earth. We know that Jesus is the Resurrection and the Life! In Jesus' name we come to you, amen.

Chapter 19: Passion Week Part 1

(What you will need: large bowl of warm water, towel)

Review: Jesus had a very busy week. First, he visited his friend, Lazarus, whom he had raised from the dead. That was amazing! Everyone should have been very happy because Jesus had raised Lazarus from the dead. Mary and Martha were happy. The disciples were happy.

Lesson: But some people were not happy. Do you know who they were? They were the religious leaders in Jerusalem, two miles away. They were angry! Many people who once followed the religious leaders had gone to follow Jesus. They believed that Jesus was the Promised One because of that miracle. The leaders were jealous of Jesus.

"We must kill Jesus!" they decided. "Everyone is following him! And we need to kill Lazarus, too. People believe in Jesus because of him." So the priests and their helpers began to plot to kill Jesus.

But Jesus was unstoppable! One day he asked his disciples to borrow a donkey. Jesus sat on the donkey and rode from Bethany to Jerusalem. Crowds followed him calling out, "Hosanna!" That means hurray! "Hosanna! Blessed is he who comes in the name of the Lord! Hosanna to the Son of David"

You see, there was a prophecy in the Holy Scriptures that said, "See, your king comes to you, righteous and having salvation, gentle and riding on a donkey." The people of Bethany and Jerusalem knew about that prophecy. Here was their King! They waved palm branches all around him and threw their coats down on the ground for the donkey to walk on. The children and their parents shouted, "Hosanna! Hosanna!"

Jesus rode right through the gates of Jerusalem and went into the great temple. He got off the donkey and went inside. The first room of the temple was supposed to be a place where people from other places could come and learn about God and pray. It was the week of the Passover Feast, when people came from all over to offer animal sacrifices to God at the temple. Some shopkeepers had found a way to make money from the visitors. They brought animals right into the prayer room and were selling them there! They were even cheating the people who came, charging them a lot of money for the animals. There was no quiet place for people to pray. There was even smelly animal poop on the floor!

Jesus was angry. He braided some rope together and made a whip. Then he began whipping the moneychangers, tipping over their tables, and sending the animals and birds out of the temple. Jesus shouted, "It is written in the Scriptures, 'My house shall be a house of prayer!' But you have turned it into a den of thieves!"

The shopkeepers and moneychangers fled from the temple. Animals ran out and birds flew outside, too. Finally! People now had a quiet place to pray.

The children who had followed Jesus shouted, "Hosanna to the Son of David! Hosanna! Hosanna!" With the temple cleared, people came to Jesus. They brought those who were sick and Jesus healed them.

After that, Jesus and his disciples walked toward a house where they had rented a room. Soon the disciples began to quietly argue among themselves as they walked along the dusty road. One of them said, "When Jesus is King, I want to be the second in command!"

"No! I want to be Jesus' second in command!" whispered another. They all began to argue about why each one of them should be more important than the others! But they did it quietly so Jesus wouldn't hear them.

But Jesus knew what they were saying. He called them together and said, "In the kingdoms of this world, those who are leaders are very bossy toward others and tell them what to do. But in MY kingdom, it is not like that at all. In MY kingdom, the greatest is the one who serves everyone else. The person who is first in line will become the last, and the last will become the first."

When they reached the house where they were staying, Jesus took a bowl of water and picked up a towel. He went up to one disciple and knelt at his feet. He took the man's sandals off and lifted the feet into the water. Then he gently washed off all the dust from the road and dried the disciple's feet. He washed all the disciples' feet!

They were shocked! Jesus was the great King! What was he doing? Only servants washed people's feet! They didn't know what to say. When he had finished, Jesus smiled and said, "Do you understand what I have just done? I, your Teacher and Lord have washed your feet. I have set an example for you. If I, your Master, have washed your feet, then you should wash each other's feet, too."

Jesus did this to show that he wants us to serve each other, not boss each other around. When we help others and serve them, we give Jesus a happy heart.

Memory Maker: Let's pretend we are with Jesus and the disciples. Each of you sit on a chair. *(Bring out a large bowl of warm water and a towel. Wash each child's feet. If they are wearing long stockings, just wash their hands. When you are all finished, ask...)* This is one way Jesus said we can serve one another. Can you think of other ways we can help people?

Prayer: Dear Father in Heaven, thank you that Jesus showed us how to serve others. Help us to look for ways we can help others every day! In Jesus' name, amen.

Chapter 20: Passion Week Part 2

(What you will need: blue removable sticky putty or removable black sticky dots)

Review: In our last lesson, we learned how Jesus rode into Jerusalem on a donkey and people called, "Hosanna! Blessed is he who comes in the name of the Lord!" All the people who followed Jesus thought he would become their King. Then Jesus went to the temple. What did he do there? *(He drove out the people who were selling animals. He said, "My house shall be called a house of prayer!" Then he healed people.)* When Jesus' disciples were arguing about who would be the greatest, what did Jesus do? *(He washed their feet, like a servant would. He told them to serve one another.)*

Lesson: The same night that Jesus washed the disciples' feet to teach them how to serve one another, Jesus told his disciples that the religious leaders would kill him. He was going to die for the sins of all the people in the world. But afterward, he said, he would rise again from the dead on the third day.

All the disciples heard was that Jesus was going to die! They were very upset!

Later that evening, the religious leaders sent soldiers to capture Jesus. The soldiers took him to the chief priest, King Herod and to the Romans. They told everyone that Jesus was bad and that he claimed to be the King of the Jews.

The next day, the Roman soldiers beat Jesus. They took him out to a hill called Calvary. They stripped off his robe and nailed him to a cross. Above Jesus' head, they nailed a sign that said, "Jesus, King of the Jews".

Mary, Jesus' mother, and her sister watched the Romans crucify Jesus. John stood next to Jesus' mother. Mary, the wife of Cleopas, Mary Magdalene and some other women were there with them. Their hearts were broken. How could the religious leaders do this to their Jesus? He was kind and gentle and good!

But this was all part of God's plan. You see, God loved everyone on earth so much, that he had made a way to rescue them from the Sin Trap. If someone perfect would take the punishment for the sins of those who were caught in the Sin Trap, that perfect person could open the trap and get people out! When Jesus, who was perfect, was on that cross, God put all the bad things done by all the people in the world on Jesus.

Memory Maker: What were some of the sins God put on Jesus that day? (Name some of the sins, large and small.) Each one of us disobeys God sometimes, too. But God put our sins on Jesus. (Each one put a black dot or sticky putty on Jesus' body in the picture where he's on the cross. Teacher goes first, followed by each child. As they put the mark on the picture, say,) "That mark is all the bad things (I/you) have ever done or ever will do."

The sky grew dark like midnight. Everyone was scared! Jesus cried out, "It is finished!" Then he died. What did he mean when he said that it was finished? He meant that everything he had to do in order to rescue us was done! The sun slowly came out again. Jesus' mother and his friends saw that he was dead. They cried. One of the Roman soldiers said, "Surely, this was the Son of God! He was innocent!"

Then some men who were friends of Jesus took him down off the cross and carried his body to a tomb - a grave - in a garden. It was not a grave in the ground. It was a cave. They wrapped Jesus body in a long, white piece of cloth and covered his face with a smaller piece of cloth. Jesus' friends went out of the cave and rolled a big stone across the opening.

Back in Jerusalem, the religious leaders went to the Roman leader, Pilate, and said, "This man Jesus said that he would rise from the dead in three days. We want you to send some guards out to his grave. That way, Jesus' disciples can't steal his body and say that Jesus rose from the dead."

So Pilate sent Roman soldiers out to guard the tomb.

The next day was the Sabbath, the day of rest. Jesus' friends cried and mourned for him that day. They forgot that Jesus said he would rise again from the dead! In our next story, we will see what happened!

Prayer: Dear Jesus, thank you for dying for my sins. I love you so much! Amen.

Chapter 21: Passion Week Part 3

(What you will need: a table with a blanket hung over the side; 2-3 baskets with potpourri or dried flowers or little bags of cinnamon sticks in them)

Review: Do you remember what happened to Jesus in our last lesson? *(He was crucified.)* What did God put on Jesus while he was on the cross? *(All our sins and all the sins of everyone in the world.)* After Jesus died, his friends put him in a tomb. Who stood guard at the tomb? *(Roman soldiers.)*

Lesson: Do you think that Roman soldiers could keep Jesus in the grave if he rose from the dead? No! On Sunday, very early in the morning before it was light, Jesus' mother, Mary, and some of the women went to the tomb to put spices on Jesus' body to make it smell good.

Memory Maker: Let's pretend we are taking spices to Jesus' grave with them. *(Give each child a small bag or container with a little bit of spice or potpourri in it)* Now let's go to the tomb. *(Lead the way to the table with a blanket hung over it.)* Oh! An angel! Look how bright he is! He's like lightening! Look! The Roman soldiers are scared! They are falling to the ground! The angel said, "Jesus is not here - he has risen, just as he said! Come, look in the grave and see where he used to be!" *(Move the blanket to the side.)* Look! The angel is rolling away the stone! Oh, look! The grave is empty! The angel said, "Go tell Jesus' disciples that he is risen!" *(Send children back to their seats.)*

The women were excited, but afraid. They stopped at the house where the disciples were and told them what the angel said. But the disciples didn't believe them.

Mary Magdalene went to the tomb alone. She was very sad and was crying. When she reached the tomb, she looked inside. Jesus wasn't there! Mary ran back to the room where Peter and the other disciples were. She said, "Somebody has taken Jesus' body away!"

Peter and John looked at each other. They jumped up and ran to the garden. Mary followed them, but she couldn't keep up.

When Peter and John reached the tomb, they looked inside. There on the shelf where Jesus' body had been lay the white grave clothes. Neatly folded next to it was the cloth that had been over Jesus' face. But Jesus' body wasn't there!

Peter and John walked slowly back to the house. Could it be true? Was Jesus alive?

Mary came to the grave last. She was crying. She looked inside the tomb and there were two angels! They said, "Why are you crying?"

Mary said, "Someone has taken away my Lord, and I do not know where they have laid him."

She put her hands up to her face and cried harder. She turned. She saw a man standing there. Was it the gardener?

The man said, "Why are you crying? Whom are you seeking?"

Mary said, "Sir, if you have carried Jesus away, tell me where you have put him and I will take him away."

Then the man said, "Mary!"

She knew that voice! Mary turned and wiped the tears from her eyes. It was Jesus! "Jesus! Teacher!" she cried. She ran toward him.

Jesus smiled and said, "Mary, don't hug me yet! I need to go to God my Father first. But I want you to go tell my disciples that I am alive."

Do you think Mary was excited? Yes! She was! She ran back to the house and told the disciples, "Jesus is alive! I have seen him!"

Some of the disciples believed her, but some of them did not. This was too amazing! Let's thank God for this!

Prayer: Dear Father God, Thank you that Jesus chose to be punished for all the bad things we have done, and thank you for raising Jesus, from the dead! We know this means that you forgive our sins when we believe in Jesus. Thank you! In Jesus' name, amen.

Chapter 22: Road To Emmaus

(What you will need: sticky putty; Sin Trap container with hearts in it. Make sure each child's name is on a heart, and put hearts in the Sin Trap.)

Review: It had been a sad and confusing week for Jesus' disciples. First, Jesus had been welcomed as the King in Jerusalem. Then the religious leaders had him arrested and crucified! Jesus died on a cross! Everyone who loved Jesus was sad. But then Mary Magdalene told the disciples that Jesus had risen from the dead! Was it true?

Lesson: Two of Jesus' followers were walking home from Jerusalem on the day Jesus rose from the dead. The Bible tells us that one of them was named Cleopas, but it does not tell us the name of the other person. Many people think the other person was his wife, Mary. So we will call her Mary. As Cleopas and Mary were walking to their home in the little town of Emmaus, they talked about what had happened. They were very confused.

They didn't notice the man coming alongside them at first. The man was Jesus, but God didn't let them recognize him. "What are you talking about?" the man asked.

"Haven't you heard?" Cleopas said. "Jesus of Nazareth, the great prophet and teacher was in Jerusalem. He did mighty miracles, but the religious leaders captured him and had him crucified! We had hoped that Jesus was the Promised One." Cleopas sighed. "But then something strange happened. Some women who followed Jesus went to his tomb this morning and found it empty. They claim that an angel told them Jesus had risen from the dead! Some of the men went there to check, and the body was gone. We don't know what to think!"

Jesus smiled. He said, "Don't you know that the Holy Scriptures say that the Promised One would have to suffer and die before he became King?"

Cleopas and Mary must have looked surprised.

"Yes!" Jesus said. "Isaiah the prophet wrote that God the Father would put the sins of the whole world on the Promised One. Remember what else Isaiah wrote? He said that the Promised One did nothing wrong and never lied to anyone. Yet he would be punished for our sins. Then he would be laid in a rich man's tomb. Wasn't Jesus put in a rich man's tomb?"

"Why, yes!" Cleopas said eagerly. "He was put in the tomb belonging to Joseph of Arimathea, a secret follower of Jesus, a very rich man!"

Jesus said, "Isaiah also said that because the Promised One would be punished for the sins of others, God would forgive the sins of all those who believe in him! And don't you remember that David said he would rise again from the dead?"

Cleopas and Mary were very excited now.

Jesus told them about other prophecies in the Bible that talked about him, too. The more he said, the happier the two disciples grew. Finally, they reached Cleopas' and Mary's home. Jesus waved good-bye and started on. But they called him back. "Please! Stay with us and have dinner!"

When they went inside, they sat down at the table. Jesus blessed the bread for them, and suddenly, they recognized him! It was Jesus! Wow! They were so excited!

So Cleopas and Mary ate quickly and hurried back to Jerusalem to tell the others. It was a long way to go, but they just had to tell everyone. Those who followed Jesus and most of the lead disciples were together in an upper room of an inn, a motel. Cleopas and Mary knocked on the door.

One of the disciples opened the door carefully. Everyone was afraid of the religious leaders. Would soldiers come to get the disciples, too? When the disciple saw who it was, he let them inside.

"Jesus is alive! We saw him!" Cleopas and Mary told the other disciples.

Just then, Jesus appeared in the room! He didn't have to come through the door or anything. He just appeared. But the other disciples were afraid. They thought Jesus was a ghost!

Jesus said, "Why are you afraid? It is I, Jesus! Here. Look at my hands and feet where the nails from the cross were. Touch me! Ghosts don't have bodies like I do. I'm for real!" Jesus held out his hands and showed them the marks from the nails. Then he put out his feet for them to see.

The disciples could hardly believe it! They were filled with joy! Jesus explained to them all about why he had to die for the sins of the world. Then Jesus said, "I want you to tell the whole world about this! Tell everyone that I will forgive all the sins of everyone who asks to be forgiven and turns away from sin."

Memory Maker: (Hold up Sin Trap.) Jesus has power over the Sin Trap. When we give him our hearts, Jesus tells Satan, "That person gave me his heart. He's mine! Let him go!" Then Jesus opens the Sin Trap, takes our heart out of the trap, and shuts the lid behind us. (Demonstrate.) We can never go back into the Sin Trap. From now on, we belong to Jesus! Do you want Jesus to rescue your heart from the Sin Trap? If you do, pray with me: "Dear Jesus, thank you for dying to rescue me from the Sin Trap! I love you so much and I give you my heart. Help me to live for you always. Amen." (Now have children come forward one at a time. Take their hearts out of the Sin Trap and have them put their hearts around the picture of Jesus with sticky putty.) If you have given your hearts to Jesus, you belong to him now. He loves you so much! And he will always watch over you and protect you and show you how to live for him.

Chapter 23: The Meeting At Galilee

(What you will need: artificial or pretend campfire; basket that contains goldfish crackers, or you can use bits of tuna in little cups -- one for each child; juice or water.)

Review: What a busy time the disciples of Jesus were having! First, Jesus was captured by the religious leaders and crucified on a cross. But then Jesus rose from the dead! Wow! What did it all mean? Jesus spent a lot of time telling them that this was God's Rescue Plan to save people from the Sin Trap. Because Jesus was punished for our sins, anyone who believes in him and gives Jesus their soul-hearts will be set free from the Sin Trap! That means that someday they can go to Heaven to be with God, who loves us so much.

Lesson: Does this mean that we will never do anything bad again? No. Sometimes we will still do bad things. But when we do, we say, "Jesus, I was bad. Will you please forgive me? Will you please help me to do what is right? And he will, because he loves us so much.

After Jesus rose from the dead, he told his disciples to meet him in Galilee. So they all went back to the area round the Sea of Galilee to wait for Jesus. While they were waiting, Peter said, "I'm going fishing."

"Me too! Me too!" said some of the other disciples. So they went out to Peter's boat and sailed onto the sea. It was growing dark when they left, because that was the best time to catch fish. All night long they cast their nets into the water. But it was not a good night for them. Not even one fish got caught in their nets.

When the sun started to come up in the morning, the disciples sailed back toward shore. While they were still a ways out, they saw a man standing on the shore. The man called, "Did you catch any fish?"

"No!" they shouted.

"Try casting your nets on the right-hand side of the boat," the man called.

The disciples gathered their nets and threw them into the water on the right-hand side of the boat. The nets were suddenly filled with fish! The catch was huge! But the nets didn't break.

John looked at the man on the shore. He remembered a time three years before when Jesus had told them the same thing, and they had a huge catch of fish. That must be Jesus on the shore! John looked at Peter and said, "It's the Lord!"

Peter looked toward the shore. Yes! That was Jesus! He jumped out of the boat and swam to shore. Do you think he hugged Jesus? I think he did! Maybe Jesus got all wet from that hug, too.

The other disciples brought the boat in. They hopped out of the boat and waded toward Jesus. There on the sand was a campfire with fish roasting over it. Jesus had breakfast all ready!

"Go bring in the fish you caught," Jesus said.

Peter went back to the boat and hauled in the nets full of fish. The disciples counted them. There were 153 large fish. What a catch!

"Let's eat breakfast now," Jesus said. This was the third time Jesus had appeared to them since he had been raised from the dead.

During breakfast, Jesus had a long talk with Peter. He asked, "Do you love me, Peter?"

Peter said, "Yes, I love you, Lord!"

Jesus said, "Then feed my sheep." Jesus wanted Peter to look after those who believed in him. Peter was to take care of them. He was to teach them the things Jesus had taught. Peter was to be a leader among the Christians. It was a big job, but Jesus knew Peter could do it.

Jesus gives each of us jobs to do for him. Jesus wants some to become Bible teachers. Some are to help other people with things they need. Others are to preach. Some people pray for others to be healed and they ask God for miracles. Some write songs and lead in singing. Everyone in Jesus' church has something to do for him. Every person's job is important to Jesus. How do we know what our job is? When we give our hearts to Jesus, he gives us a special gift. God the Holy Spirit comes to live in our hearts. The Holy Spirit helps us know what job we are supposed to do for Jesus.

Memory Maker: Let's pretend we are with the disciples and Jesus and eat breakfast with them. *(Set up an artificial fire pit or just pretend you have a fire. Have the children sit around fire in a circle. Pass goldfish crackers or tuna, and juice, around to each child.)* What kind of things do you want to do for Jesus? *(Encourage each child to say what he/she would like to do.)*

Prayer: Dear Father in Heaven, thank you for giving us the Holy Spirit to teach us about Jesus. Help us to listen closely to what your Word, the Bible, tells us about you, and help us choose to trust and obey you always. In Jesus' name, amen.

Chapter 24: Jesus Goes Back To Heaven

(What you will need: Blue cloth in the shape of a pond; fishing poles with magnets on the end of the line; cut-out hearts with paper clips attached; picture of God on his throne from Lesson One.)

Review: Jesus did so many things in just a few days! He died on a cross and took the punishment for all the sins of the world. He was put in a tomb with Roman soldiers guarding it, but God raised him from the dead on the third day!

Lesson: The religious leaders back in Jerusalem were very upset about this! The Roman soldiers told them about the angel that rolled away the stone at the tomb, and that Jesus wasn't inside. The religious leaders told the soldiers, "Look, we'll pay you a lot of money if you will tell people that you fell asleep and that Jesus' disciples stole his body!" So that's what the soldiers did.

There was just one problem: Jesus kept appearing to people! The Bible tells us that Jesus appeared to five hundred people! Everyone was talking about it!

Jesus met with all his friends and disciples. He appeared to Peter three times, because Peter would be the leader of those who followed Jesus. When Jesus met with his disciples, he told them that he was going back to heaven soon. The disciples remembered that Jesus had told them this once before. Jesus had said, "I am going away to my Father. But don't be sad! In my Father's house are many rooms. I'm going to prepare rooms for you!"

Do you remember those pictures of heaven we saw? *(Show pictures of God's throne from Chapter One.)* Remember that God's throne is at the center of Heaven, and that angels fly around him day and night? This is the wonderful place Jesus is preparing for us!

Finally the day came for Jesus to go back to Heaven. Jesus told his disciples to go out to a hill. He met them there. He had one last thing to tell them. It was very important!

Jesus looked at his disciples and smiled. He said, "All power in heaven and earth has been given to me. So here's what I want you to do: Go out into the whole world and tell everyone about me! Tell everyone about how I came to earth to rescue them from the Sin Trap. Tell them I took the punishment for their sins when I died on the cross. Tell them that God raised me from the dead three days later! Tell everyone that if they believe in me, they can live with me forever in Heaven! When people believe in me, baptize them in the name of the Father and the Son and the Holy Spirit.

"And listen: I will be with you always! I will be with you to the end of time! Now, go!"

Suddenly Jesus started moving up into a cloud! The cloud came all around him, and the disciples couldn't see him anymore. The disciples remembered that Jesus had told them he would return to earth after they had told the whole world about him. So they needed to get busy! They looked hard at that cloud. They couldn't see Jesus anymore.

An angel appeared in front of the disciples. "Men of Galilee, why are you standing here looking up into the sky? Don't you know that Jesus is going to come back to earth the same way he left it?"

In the Book of Revelation, the last book of the Bible, John tells us that Jesus will return in the clouds, riding a white horse. When Jesus comes back, he will rescue us from all the bad people who don't love him. He will give us a home with him forever. When Jesus comes back there will no longer be anymore pain or sadness. There will only be happiness! For God will be with us forever.

Prayer: Dear Father in Heaven, thank you for sending Jesus to teach us about you! Help us to tell everyone we know about Jesus so that they can live in Heaven someday, too. In Jesus' name, amen.

Memory Maker: Jesus said we are supposed to tell everyone about him. Do you have friends who don't know about Jesus? Today we are going to practice telling them a little bit about Jesus. *(Put blue pond on floor, bring out fishing poles and paper hearts.)* Let's pretend these hearts are our friends. You will put your fishing pole over the hearts and say the name of one of your friends. Then say, "Jesus loves you!" or "I gave my heart to Jesus. So can you!" Then we will catch a heart and pull it out of the pond. Remember how Jesus told us to be fishers of men? Fishers of people? This is how we do it: We tell others about Jesus.

Teacher's Guide

The Prince And The Plan is designed for parents to use at home as well as for children's ministry teachers. For those who use this material in a classroom setting, I have included song suggestions and memory verses that can be used to supplement the lessons. For those who would like to know the Biblical foundation for these lessons, I have listed the portions of Scripture that I used in preparing this book.

At the end of the Teacher's Guide I have included activities you might enjoy using that will reinforce the Bible lessons.

Chapter 1: How It All Began

Suggested song: God Is So Good; Awesome God
Memory verse: 1 John 1:5
Bible references:
1 John 1:5 tells us that God is light.
John 4:24 - God is a spirit
John 1:18 - No man has seen God - only Jesus has (this refers to physical sight; some have seen God while in the spirit.)
Isaiah 6:1-3 tells us that God allowed Isaiah to see him in the spirit realm through a vision.
Revelation 4:3 describes God on his throne the way the Apostle John saw him.
Revelation 21:1-22:5 describes what the God on his throne will look like when he brings the New Jerusalem to earth.
1 John 5:14 reports that God hears us when we pray.
Romans 8:28 tells us that God makes all things work together for good for those who love him. Evil men and angels may have bad designs and hurt us, but God takes what happens and turns it into something that will benefit us and bring great glory to himself.
Psalm 91:11 states that God sends his angels to watch over us.
Matthew 18:10 refers to the angels of children.

(On the Holy Trinity)
Isaiah 9:6 tells us that the Promised One (Jesus) will be God
John 1:1-3 reports that Jesus is God the Creator
Matthew 28:18-20 - Jesus commands baptism in the name of the Father, the Son and the Holy Spirit, indicating Holy Trinity.

Chapter 2: Creation And Hearts

Suggested song: This Is My Father's World; God Is So Good
Memory verse: Genesis 1:1
Bible references:
(On interpretation of Genesis)
Many Christians in our nation no longer believe that Genesis is a literal account. However, Jesus, the Creator (John 1:3; Colossians 1:16-19) referred to events in Genesis as fact. (Mark 10:6; Luke 11:49-51; Matthew 24:37-39, and multiple other verses). The Apostles also believed Genesis was literal. (Hebrews 11:1-22; Jude verses 5-11, 14; Acts 7:2-14; Acts 14:15) Genesis is mentioned 103 times in the New Testament. This implies that Genesis actually happened the way it is recorded in the Bible. If it were not so, Jesus and the Apostles would have told us. By faith, that is the position I am taking in teaching Genesis.

(On the human soul)
Genesis 2:7 tells us that God formed Adam - in the image and likeness of God - out of the dust of the earth, then breathed into him, and Adam became a living "soul" (KJV). The soul sets man apart from animals. We have purpose! The Bible speaks of man's soul as his "heart". (Prov. 16:1, 5, 9, 21, 23; Jeremiah 17:9)

(On history of Satan)
When Ezekiel was prophesying against the king of Tyre in Ezekiel 28, he compared the king's attitude to Satan in verses 11-17a. Here we have the most complete account of Satan's existence. Many think this passage refers to Satan, not the king of Tyre, because of several statements: "You were in Eden" - verse 13. "You were the anointed cherub who covers" - verse 14. "...I cast you as profane from the mountain of God" - verse 16 (NASB).
Revelation 12:7-11 gives a detailed account of Satan being cast out of heaven by Michael, the archangel, leader of God's army.
Isaiah 14:12-16 paints a similar picture that many Bible scholars believe compares the king of Babylon to Satan. Some versions give Satan his original name: Lucifer.

Chapter 3: The Choice

Suggested song: Every Promise In The Book Is Mine; This Is My Father's World
Memory verse: Psalm 62:6
Bible References:
Genesis 3:1-7 - This passage speaks of how Satan divided mankind from God. (See Chapter 2 for history of Satan) We know from later Scripture that Satan possessed the body of the serpent and tempted Eve to disobey God. He lied to her about supposed advantages she would have if she ate the forbidden fruit. Eve was deceived. Adam chose

to eat the fruit, too, but he was not deceived.
2 Timothy 2:14; Romans 5:12 --The result was that sin entered the world. The Bible places the blame squarely on Adam, who willfully and knowingly sinned.

(On the Sin Trap)
2 Timothy 2:26 - The Bible speaks of "the snare of the devil". A snare is a trap. I have chosen this word picture to help children visualize the problem of sin.
1 Corinthians 15:22; Psalm 51:5; Romans 3:11-12, 23 - Everyone is born a sinner, inside the Sin Trap.

(On pre-creation plan of salvation)
1 Peter 1:20 & Revelation 13:8 tells us that before God created the world, Jesus was already chosen to die for us, to rescue us from the penalty of sin.

Chapter 4: God Plans A Rescue
Suggested songs: Jesus Loves Me; King of Kings & Lord of Lords
Memory verse: John 3:16
Bible references:
Genesis 3:8-24 - Tells of the consequences of Adam's and Eve's disobedience.
Micah 5:2 - Prophecy of where the Promised One (Jesus) would be born.
Isaiah 7:14 - This prophecy indicates that the Promised One would be born of a virgin.
Numbers 24:17 - The prophecy here indicates that the Promised One will be a descendant of Jacob (Israel), and that he will be a King.
John 3:16 - This verse tells how God fulfilled his promise to Adam and Eve.

Chapter 5: God Plans A Rescue
Suggested songs: Emmanuel (His name is called Emmanuel); Awesome God
Memory verse: Matthew 1:21
Bible references:
Matthew 1:18-25 tells the story for this lesson.
John 1:1-4 speaks of Jesus' pre-existence as a Spirit and of his taking on human flesh.
Isaiah 7:14 is the prophecy of Jesus' virgin birth.

Chapter 6: What Happened At Bethlehem
Suggested songs: Away In A Manger; Emmanuel
Memory verse: Luke 2:11
Bible references:
Luke 2:1-20 tells the story for this lesson.
Numbers 24:17 tells of the star God would place in the sky to announce Jesus' birth.

Chapter 7: The Wise Men

Suggested songs: We Three Kings of Orient Are; King of Kings and Lord of Lords
Memory verse: Matthew 2:2
Bible references:
Matthew 2:1-18 tells the story of the visit from the wise men.
Numbers 24:17 tells of the star God would place in the sky to announce Jesus' birth.
Matthew 2:7 tells us that Herod learned of the time the star appeared. His actions in Matthew 2:16 indicate that he knew Jesus was two years old or younger at the time of the wise men's visit.

Chapter 8: What Jesus Learned in School

Suggested songs: The B-I-B-L-E; ABC Jesus Loves Me
Memory verse: Luke 2:52
Background: Information for what Jesus learned in school can be supported by historical records of what the Jewish people taught their sons. We know that Jesus could both read and write, for he demonstrated it. We also know that Jesus was thoroughly trained in knowledge of the Holy Scriptures. Jesus demonstrated great knowledge of the books of the Old Testament.
Bible references:
Exodus 1 & 2 tell the story of how the Israelis became slaves in Egypt, and the birth of Moses, who would rescue them.
Exodus 3:7-10 tells that God heard Israel's cry for deliverance.
Exodus 4:18-12:42 tells the story of how God delivered Israel from Egypt.
Exodus 20:1-17 lists the Ten Commandments God gave to Moses.
Matthew 22:34-40 - Jesus tells the purpose of the commandments.

Chapter 9: John Baptizes Jesus

Suggested song: I Have Decided To Follow Jesus
Memory verse: John 1:29
Background: Historically, it is thought that John the Baptist's parents, who were quite old at his birth, were dead by the time John began his ministry at age 30.
Bible references:
Matthew 3:1-17; Mark 1:1-11; Luke 3:1-23 and John 1:15-34 all tell about John the Baptist's work and the baptism of Jesus.

Chapter 10: Fishers of Men

Suggested song: I Will Make You Fishers of Men; I Have Decided To Follow Jesus
Memory verse: Matthew 4:19
Bible references:

Luke 5:1-11; Matthew 4:18-22 and Mark 1:14-20 tell the story for this lesson.

Chapter 11: The Sermon On The Mount Part 1
Suggested songs: If You're Happy And You Know It; Awesome God
Memory verse: Matthew 19:14
Bible references:
Matthew 5:1-12 lists the Beatitudes.
Matthew 19:13-15 and Luke 18:15-17 both record the story of Jesus blessing the children.

Chapter 12: The Sermon On The Mount Part 2
Suggested song: This Is My Father's World; If You're Happy And You Know It
Memory verse: Matthew 6:33
Bible references:
Matthew 6:25-30 and John 6:1-13 tell the events in this lesson.

Chapter 13: The Grateful Leper
Suggested songs: Thank You, Jesus (Christian Kids Praise); Open The Eyes of My Heart, Lord
Suggested memory verse: Psalm 106:1
Background: Leviticus 13:1-46. Historically, lepers were forced to live outside the towns of Israel, in caves or shelters they built themselves. Leprosy was a contagious disease and considered incurable. Usually caused by nutritional deficiencies and exposure to cold, it ravaged bodies.
Bible references:
Luke 17:11-17 tells the story of how Jesus healed the lepers.

Chapter 14: Jairus' Daughter
Suggested songs: Wonderful, Wonderful, Isn't He Wonderful; I Want To Praise You Lord, Much More Than I Do (Randy Thomas, Sam O. Scott)
Suggested memory verse: Matthew 7:7
Bible references:
Luke 8:40-56 tells the story of Jairus' daughter.
Proverbs 3:5,6 tells us to trust the Lord, not ourselves.

Chapter 15: Jesus Visits Friends
Suggested songs: Open The Eyes of My Heart, Lord; I Want To Praise You Lord Much More Than I Do (by Randy Thomas, Sam O. Scott)
Suggested memory verse: Exodus 15:26 (last part)

Bible references:
Luke 10:38-41 tells the story of Jesus' visit with Mary, Martha & Lazarus.

Chapter 16: Jesus Calms Storms And Casts Out Demons
Suggested songs: I've Got Peace Like A River; I've Got The Joy, Joy, Joy
Suggested memory verse: Isaiah 26:3
Bible references:
Mark 4:35-5:20 tells the story for this lesson.

Chapter 17: Jesus And Peter Walk On Water
Suggested songs: God Can Do Anything But Fail; Every Promise In The Book Is Mine
Suggested memory verse: Matthew 19:26, last part
Bible references: Matthew 14:22-36 tells the story of Jesus and Peter walking on water.

Chapter 18: Jesus Raises Lazarus
Suggested songs: Awesome God; King of Kings & Lord of Lords
Suggested memory verse: John 11:25, first half
Bible references:
John 11:1-44 tells the story of Lazarus being raised from the dead.
1 Thessalonians 4:16-18 speaks of the resurrection of the dead.
Revelation 21:1-4 tells us that someday, when God lives among us, there will be no more death.

Chapter 19: Passion Week Part 1
Suggested songs: King of Kings & Lord of Lords; If You Wanna Be Great In God's Kingdom
Suggested memory verse: Galatians 5:13, last phrase
Bible references:
Matthew 21:1-17 tells the story of Jesus triumphal entry to Jerusalem.
Zechariah 9:9 predicts Christ's triumphal entry to Jerusalem on a donkey.
Isaiah 56:7 is the verse Jesus quoted about God's house being a place of prayer.
Luke 22:24-27 - Jesus instructs the disciples on being servant-leaders.
John 13:1-17 talks about Jesus washing his disciples feet.

Chapter 20: Passion Week Part 2
Suggested songs: I Want To Praise You Lord; Thank You, Jesus
Suggested memory verse: Isaiah 53:6
Bible references:
Matthew 26 & 27 tell the story of the Last Supper, Jesus' arrest, trial and crucifixion.

Mark 14 & 15; Luke 22 & 23; John 18 & 19 all tell the story for this lesson.

Isaiah 53 is the Old Testament prediction of Jesus' life, death for the sins of mankind, and burial.

Matthew 16:21 - Jesus told his disciples he would be killed, then rise again on the third day.

Chapter 21: Passion Week Part 3

Suggested songs: Awesome God; Open the Eyes of My Heart, Lord

Suggested memory verse: Matthew 28:5

Bible references:

Matthew 28:10-12; Mark 16:1-11; Luke 24:1-12 and John 20:1-18 record the resurrection of Jesus from the dead.

Chapter 22: Road To Emmaus

Suggested songs: Wonderful, Wonderful, Isn't He Wonderful? If You're Happy And You Know It

Suggested memory verse: John 3:16

Bible references:

Luke 24:13- 49 - Tells the story of the road to Emmaus and Jesus' appearance to the disciples.

Isaiah 53 is the longest Old Testament prophecy of the life, death, burial and resurrection of Jesus.

Psalm 16:10 prophesies that Jesus would rise again from the dead.

John 3:16 & 17 tell why God sent Jesus into the world.

John 10:28-30 speaks of the eternal security of those who believe in Jesus.

Romans 8:2 speaks of how Jesus set us free from the curse that came on humanity when Adam and Eve disobeyed God, and the curse of disobeying the commandments given in Exodus, Leviticus, Numbers & Deuteronomy.

I John 1:9 instructs us to confess our sins and Jesus will forgive us.

Chapter 23: The Meeting At Galilee

Suggested songs: Fishers of Men; Every Promise In The Book Is Mine

Suggested memory verse: 1 Corinthians 12:7 (suggest New Living Translation)

Bible references:

John 21:1-15 tells the story for this lesson.

1 Corinthians 12 & 13 speak of the gifts of the Holy Spirit.

Chapter 24: Jesus Goes Back To Heaven

Suggested songs: (chorus) Coming Again; Fishers of Men

Suggested memory verse: Matthew 28:19

Bible references:

Acts 1:1-11 tells of Jesus' return to Heaven.

1 Corinthians 2:9 tells us that God's reward for us is unimaginably awesome.

John 14:15-21- Jesus promises to send the Holy Spirit to teach us what we need to know.

Isaiah 6:1-3 tells about God on his throne.

Revelation 21 & 22 describe the New Jerusalem and God's throne.

Revelation 19:11-16 - prophecy about Jesus' return to earth, riding a white horse.

Extra Review Activities

Review: The Fishing Game

It is good to have a question-and-answer game every four or five lessons. This one is The Fishing Game. To do this game, make fishing poles out of sticks with string, and put a magnet on the end of the string. Cut out some fish shapes (about 4 inches long) from colorful paper. Put a paper clip on the fish's nose.

Type or write short, simple review questions, with answers in parenthesis. Cut the questions into strips and paste or tape them on the back of the fish. (Typing the questions on blank address labels works well for this and saves time.)

Designate a fishing area. I use some blue cloth, or felt cut into the shape of a small pool.

Sample questions for ages 4-6: General Bible truth - Does Jesus love me? (yes) Specific to lesson - Who did Jesus raise from the dead? (Lazarus, Jairus' daughter) Keep the questions simple for the younger ones. You can use different colors of fish for each age group if you want harder questions for the older children.

Spread the fish out on the pool. Let the children take turns catching the fish with their poles. Teacher: Read the question on the fish to them. If they say the correct answer, the fish goes into the "keeper" pile. If they miss the answer, they have to put the fish back in the "water".

If you have more than five children in your group, you can divide them into teams for the game.

Dramatic Review: Creative Play Kit

Children love to re-create Bible stories in miniature format, so I developed a Creative Play Kit consisting of building blocks for houses and walls, artificial flowers and trees, aquarium marbles (for water effect), and wooden peg dolls. If you want the children to feel ownership of the sets, you can have them paint the wooden peg dolls (available through Amazon) with acrylic paint. Then you or another adult can coat each doll with a clear acrylic finish.

Rubberized shelf paper cut into a square makes a great base for a Creative Play Kit. I use green. Have the children build a scene from your story and move the peg people around to reenact the lesson. I usually let 3 or 4 children work together building the scene. This helps them learn team building.

About The Author

Sheri Schofield is a veteran in children's ministries. Starting as a teenager, Sheri worked with Child Evangelism Fellowship. As a freshman in high school, she taught second-grade girls' Sunday school class at Murphy Chapel, a small church in rural Oregon. During her college years, Sheri studied Theology and Christian Education of Children at Prairie Bible College and Biola University in preparation for a lifetime of working with and writing for children. While at Biola, she began developing her art skills as well. She now illustrates her own work. Her first book, *Race To Eagle Mountain,* placed third in Young Adult Fiction in the 2007 Moonbeam Children's Book Awards.

Along with her husband, Tim Schofield, M. D., Sheri has dedicated her life to serving Jesus. While Tim has helped people through his work as a physician, Sheri has used her writing and teaching skills to reach children. She has gone into many neighborhoods to teach Bible clubs and to help people in need, and has taught in local churches. When Tim served with the military in Panama in 1993-1994, Sheri home schooled their two children, Drew and Christy, and started her own radio program for the children of Panama City through HOXO Radio, a sister station of HCJB Trans World Radio in Ecuador. Later their family moved to Montana, where their children grew up and were married. Tim and Sheri have three grandchildren at this time.

Most of Sheri's work over the past two decades has been with children ages 4-8. She also developed and taught leadership training programs for children ages 7-10 and for junior high students at her home church, Helena Alliance, in Helena, Montana.